W9-BYU-875

WITHDRAWN

**Illinois Central College
Learning Resources Center**

GAYLORD

CLINT EASTWOOD
RIDING HIGH

Also by Douglas Thompson
Like a Virgin: Madonna Revealed (Smith Gryphon)

CLINT EASTWOOD
RIDING HIGH

DOUGLAS THOMPSON

CⱭB

CONTEMPORARY
BOOKS

CHICAGO

First published in Great Britain in 1992 by Smith Gryphon Limited

Copyright © 1992 by Douglas Thompson
Published by Contemporary Books, Inc.
180 North Michigan Avenue, Chicago, Illinois 60601
Manufactured in the United States of America
International Standard Book Number: 0-8092-3767-9

CONTENTS

In memory of Albert Thompson and Doreen Brown,
a couple of genuine straight-shooters

ACKNOWLEDGEMENTS

CLINT EASTWOOD is a complex gentleman. He protects his privacy but understands the worldwide interest in everything about his life; and because of this, charmingly endures the attention and the questions. For that we are grateful.

Special thanks to the clever and patient Helen Armitage who edited this biography from her cat haven in London, Jeanne Karas who helped ensure facts were facts from my madhouse office in Los Angeles and to Judith Chilcote who works worldwide wonders from her London HQ, guaranteeing her place in literary agent heaven.

Extraordinary thanks to Robert Smith who is a genuine VIP – Very Important Publisher – for his continuing faith and support.

—

Showdown

'Go ahead, make my day.'

CLINT EASTWOOD IN *SUDDEN IMPACT* IN 1983

The fog is riding in with the cool wind from the Pacific and hurling down Highway One. The tall redwoods do a ghostly disco in the headlights. This is Monterey Peninsula, State of California, United States of America, and nearly two thousand acres of it are called home by Clint Eastwood.

I had driven down from San Francisco to interview Eastwood about his 1985 film *Pale Rider*. There was only one snag – he knew nothing about this plan. It was simply on the chance that this movieland icon, one of the most liked and influential box-office stars ever, would against all the odds agree to an unofficial but in-depth conversation. He has never been known as one to chew the fat. He chews tobacco. Or gently barbecued swordfish without the lemon sauce. Or marinated chicken steamed with vegetables and washed down with a chilled glass of Anchor Steam beer. As an actor, he shoots straight. As a director, he has a formidable reputation for bringing projects in ahead of schedule and below on budget. His private life is his private life. He rarely gives inter-views and even when he does, his low-profile attitude makes his words, soft, slow and lean. He didn't make his name talking.

He accomplished that and began a billion-dollar film dynasty by forgetting to shave for a couple of days, mumbling if spoken to and shooting forty-two people in ninety-three minutes. He was paid a straight $15,000 for *A Fistful of Dollars* in 1964. By 1992 his films have earned more than $2 billion.

His success has been increased by his calculated underex-posure, by making his every appearance a celebration for his world-wide audience. He is intimidating in his reluctance about publicity unless he is controlling the format. Born in San Fran-cisco on 31 May 1930, he is crowding in on getting a pension book, but his six foot four tall frame is still rangy from his daily runs and work-outs on his black Universal exercise machine, parallel bars, weights, slantboards, two punching bags which allow for sit-ups, back lifts, bench presses and boxing routines to Bach or jazz on a Sony tape-deck.

He designed his twin-level home built out of the native red-woods and Douglas fir and circled by Monterey cypresses on the Peninsula with spectacular views of the jagged, ragged coast and out the Peninsula and along Ocean Trail you run into Carmel-by-the-Sea, one of California's most popular tourist resorts. And one of America's richest and quaintest communities. One big attraction for visitors is the Hog's Breath Inn which is co-owned by East-wood who from 1986 to 1988 earned $200 a month as the mayor. to 1988 earned $200 a month as the mayor.

Even the menu and the entrance-way are Eastwood-style. There are *Dirty Harry* (cheese) hamburgers, *Magnum Force* (hot pepper) omelettes and Eastwood's favourite *Gauntlet* (boysen-berry) cheesecake. The alley is a gun-metal colour. Am I about to make Eastwood's day? Sixteen steps take you down into the restaurant's patio with its crowd of customers and roaring fire. There's a redwood bar and above it one of these *High Noon* style clocks which ticks on and on with no sight of the Man.

Then, out of the shadows he arrives striding into view in his Nike running shoes, Levi jeans and shirt and shoulder jacket. When he glances around, his eyes narrow like blinds being drawn on a private room. I suggest we might talk and suddenly his hand goes to his side. He pulls out a fistful of dollars and says: 'Well, I better buy you a beer.'

He sits and leans back by the fire. At first, he is reluctant: 'I don't usually talk business in any form here. I'm partners with two other guys and we modelled this like an English pub – a place for folks to have a drink and enjoy themselves. Look, you see me relaxing. But everybody has to have an edge and my edge is instinct. There are always people telling me what to do, but I've always done what I felt like doing.'

He is just another customer as far as the Hog's Breath regulars are concerned. Tourists will pull out cameras and ask for autographs. He never seems concerned. 'I don't have much respect for people who look down on the public as somebody who gets in the way. After all you've just asked for it, you fought to get where you are. You just don't – you can't look down. On the other hand you want privacy too because otherwise your central nervous system goes berserk.'

Yes, he agrees we will talk. But in a moment. He has something to arrange first. Eastwood takes his beer and his charm across the patio to join a small group. One of them is a tall, stunning-looking blonde in her early thirties. The *other* Eastwood – the sexual cowboy – goes into action. When he returns to talk, a smile plays on his lips and there is a twinkle in his eye. He has made his 'arrangements'. He has always been a ladies' man. In his early army days, he would moonlight at other jobs to earn enough cash to take dates out to drive-in movies.

He could afford much, much more than that when his regular film editor Ferris Webster introduced him to a female colleague at a sound laboratory at Burbank Studios in 1978.

'Clint, I want you to meet a girl who works with me. Sally meet Clint.'

Apparently, Eastwood soared to his feet with: 'How do?'

'I just wanted to say hello,' said Sally, closing the remark with: 'Well, I have to get back.'

'Come back anytime,' said Eastwood. 'In five minutes. Are you an editor?'

'No. Accounting.'

'No. I was just about to say you had a job editing . . . .'

Webster showed his colleague out and when he returned to the room he complimented her figure. Eastwood acted upset with him: 'I didn't even notice her body. I was just looking . . . straight into her eyes.'

Another film editor made a remark and Eastwood responded: 'A nice girl for those of you who like girls. Me, I'm just a poor, unfortunate . . . asexual.'

'Sure,' said a soundman. 'He just likes fast cars.'

Eastwood reportedly got a moony grin on his face at that moment and said casually: 'Fast cars and fast women.'

Paul Lippman, a former partner of his at the Hog's Breath, has talked of his charm and style with women – girls he calls Eastwood's 'hip-pocket-rockets'. Some of them took off as remarkably as Eastwood's career. He was an original Hollywood 'hunk', a contract player who posed bare-chested for publicity pictures. Usually not with one, but two girls.

I grew up watching him as Rowdy Yates, the number two trail boss on the television series *Rawhide*. He went on to the spaghetti Westerns as the Man With No Name which provoked so much interest. But it wasn't until a screening of *Magnum Force* – the sequel to *Dirty Harry* – in New York in 1973 did I realize the phenomenal impact Eastwood was having and would have on popular culture. Everyone from President Richard Nixon to Muhammad Ali wanted Eastwood to say his trademark 'Make My Day' for them. And still do.

.　　.　　.

In 1974, I flew from London to Los Angeles with Eastwood and over the years since then have interviewed him several times. Now, I have also spoken to those who know more of the private life of Clint Eastwood. About his broken marriage. About his complex and crushing legal bust-up with his longtime lover Sondra Locke. About his secret family.

Until now, it seems, we knew all about him, but we didn't know anything about him. Eastwood is a charmer. Like Warren Beatty, he can tell you nothing but make it seem like the truth and nothing but the truth. Today, he is a Hollywood legend, one of the most consistent top attractions in the history of the movies, and on the marquee with Clark Gable and Gary Cooper and John Wayne and Paul Newman in terms of star longevity. He has also had a remarkable second career as a Casanova.

When he was elected mayor of Carmel in 1986, the town was dubbed 'Clintville' and a gift shop cashed in on the name and the business that having an international movie star as the civic leader led to. They sold Eastwood T-shirts and hats and all manner of bric-à-brac and paraphernalia that could remotely be linked to the celebrity mayor. Anything, really, they could stick his name or image on. One big seller was the 'Make My Night' panties.

—

ONE

High Plains Drifter

'I've never liked drawing attention to myself.'

CLINT EASTWOOD IN 1976

Clint Eastwood fell in love with Carmel the first time he saw it. It has been the pivotal place in his life. It looks like a film set – the impossibly sweeping ocean views, the ice plant and the Monterey cypress. Eastwood was an army private stationed close to the town at Fort Ord in 1951. It was a Saturday night when he and some friends finished too late to make the trip to the bright lights of San Francisco.

'One guy had a car and we drove to Monterey, hit a few pubs, then came over the hill to Carmel. I said to myself: if I ever have any dough, I'd like to live in this place. I fell for it in a big way: beautiful green mountains, well-timbered, coming right down to the shoreline and some clean white beaches. If I ever made a few bucks.'

Eastwood has always been passionate about what he wants. But he always seems to be calm and in control of his emotions, sending the message that the laconic screen image is also reality; he admits there is a price to pay for that:

'You do pay – sometimes it's better to get things off your chest because people get relief from that. It's like going out and yelling obscenities in the middle of the highway. You come back and say, "Aaah." I'm not afraid of showing emotions, but there are certain things I just don't enjoy sharing with everybody else. There are certain thoughts – I don't feel compelled to tell every thought that is in my mind. I know a lot of people get a catharsis, they get a release, from that and that's why psychiatrists make so much money. They can sit down and really unload, but to me I've never felt that. I don't particularly want to unload on anybody else. I always felt I could go out and walk through a field and look at the flowers and just unload to myself.'

The field and the flowers are on the outskirts of Carmel. If you live there, you must die to get out of town. There is no cemetery. There is also no mail delivery for the residents refused to put up house numbers. The post office is where they meet for a gossip. Originally, around a century ago, artists boosted the population – it's now 4825 – of the modern Carmel which was discovered in 1602 by a Carmelite friar Sebastian Vizcaino and named for his patron saint, Our Lady of Carmel. In the 1920s, city ordinances were introduced banning street lights, pavements, traffic lights and today it is still against the law to wear high heels without a licence. The artists of the past frowned on business but there are now 67 art galleries, 31 real-estate brokerages and restaurants and bars lining every street of the tiny village that sits on a slope above Monterey Bay 120 miles south of San Francisco. This is Eastwood's *Heaven-Can-Wait* place.

.   .   .

In 1930 Carmel might have been 120 light years away for Clinton Eastwood, his wife, Ruth, their daughter, Jean, and newborn son, Clinton Junior. Their son had been born on 31 May that year and there wasn't much in the bank – certainly not for trips to quaint seaside communities. 'It was my parents, my sister and me,' he recalls. And any trips that were made were out of necessity. There were many as he was growing up – another job for his father, another school for him. 'Once we moved from Sacramento to Pacific Palisades [450 miles from central California to the outskirts of Los Angeles] so that my dad could start work as a gas station [garage] attendant. It was the only job open.'

His father sold stocks and bonds; there wasn't much business in the early thirties. Eastwood is particularly proud of his parents and especially his father's work ethic. It's reflected in his life today for although one of the world's richest movie stars, he never stops work for more than a short break. He admits to being a workaholic and at one time was averaging a new film every ten months – in one thirty-month period he made six films, two of which he directed. And if you look with hindsight at his work, it is easy to recognize the Depression Day hardship and humour in films like 1982's

Honkytonk Man. But he and his sister did better than many during the bad days.

'I can't remember us being poor or suffering as children. Maybe my father did have his worries but neither Jean nor I ever knew about them. When I look back I know dad had to think pretty fast at times because there were a lot of people out of work in America around the time I was born. He often moved from one stocks and bonds company to another to try and better himself. That's why although I was born in San Francisco, my earliest memories are of living in Oakland. But it seems to me now we didn't live much in houses at all – we lived in cars. I can remember only a few of the places like Oakland and San Francisco and Sacramento – twice – and Seattle. The frustrating thing about moving around like this as a kid is that you're constantly having to make adjustments. Just as soon as I'd get to make friends in a place and start making progress at my studies, we'd be on the move again.

'It gave me a taste for living all right, but I never got those feelings of security a kid most probably needs. I was always feeling left out of things. I'd walk into a fresh school and find the standards were different or they were on different phases of a subject. So although it wasn't that I wasn't bright I was never out front. I always seemed to be running to catch up.

'That feeling has sort of stuck with me and maybe it has something to do with making me a loner – why I like driving fast and riding motorcycles fast. Since I was always the new boy on the block, I often played alone and in that situation your imagination becomes very active. You create little mythologies in your own mind. I suppose it was the best thing that happened in my youth.

'I was a constant day-dreamer. When I wasn't going crazy trying to catch up on the lessons I'd missed, I'd sit there dreamy-eyed looking out of the window. I dreamed of being a great air pilot. I rescued a lot of people from drowning. I was the world's greatest surfer. And I guess I saved more people on the operating table than any surgeon who ever lived. You name it, I thought of it. I was pretty much bottled up in those days.

'I suppose my parents guessed the way I felt at times. My father was a big man physically and had competed in both football and track. He was fond of the outdoors and he took me hunting and fishing. He also taught me to swim well. When we lived in Redding and Sacramento the Sierra Nevada Mountains were nearby and Jean and I were pretty good at skiing while we were still kids.

'At school I was never the one in the class to make things go – in the first place I was about a foot taller than the rest of the kids. There were occasions when I'd have lopped myself off at the knees if that had been possible. Then I had to go through this male thing of handing it out as well as taking it. They weren't tough guys or anything like that. I was just the odd man out – the big, silent guy.' But as many a young lady and co-star were to find out, still waters really do run deep. And often dark and secretive.

Eastwood's career was taking off in 1970 when he was interviewed in Las Vegas by a lady reporter who had been in town for several days. She is introduced and he leans forward with a handshake but no hello, just: 'Yeah, I've been watching her legs for two days.' When a blonde woman sitting across from him makes a comment he offers: 'Cool it!' The other woman is Maggie Johnson Eastwood, his now former wife. In 1970 they had been married for seventeen years. It didn't seem to cramp Eastwood's style. Not much has over the years:

'I became hooked on girls at an early age. American kids seem to start dating a lot earlier than European kids, even now. I got my first crush when I was at Glenview [at age fourteen in Oakland, California] grammar school. Her name was Joan and she was a readhead, a little teeny-bopper. What attracted me, I think, was that she was the most popular girl in class. It was actually very much a one-way situation. She never showed any signs of being intrigued with me. But for a time I stopped staring out the window and began dreaming up to the front where she was sitting. Not once did I have the courage to ask her out with me.'

He overcame his early introspection, the loner became a lone wolf, prowling alone. What helped him was something that even in all his day-dreaming he had never imagined – acting. An English teacher who he reckons was a pretty fair amateur psychologist chose him to play a rebel teenager in that year's school play. He didn't want to. Miss Jones told him he would enjoy it. He suffered through hell. He wanted to run away from school. Another pupil, his friend Harry Pendleton, was also in the play. The young Eastwood tried to talk his pal into 'vanishing' saying: 'They'll laugh at us.' Harry agreed: 'They sure will.' They planned to miss the play but next day had second thoughts. It would be easier all round if they tried to work their way through it.

'I realized at some point that all the kids in the audience were laughing with me and not at me. I suppose it was the first time I realized you could act extroverted without really being so and also that being self-confident didn't mean that people took an instant dislike to you or laughed at you. I was fifteen, but it was the day I grew up.'

And, by then, girls had taken second place in his life. For a little time, anyway.

'I still wasn't fifteen when my dad bought me my first car – an old rattle trap he'd picked-up for $25. I've never exactly led what you'd call a monastic sheltered life. The car took my mind off girls for a bit. For the next couple of years it was cars first and girls second. I wasn't actually supposed to drive on my learner's permit except in an emergency. But even at that age I was within one inch of my present height and the cops never stopped me. That summer when I was fifteen I left home for the first time. It was just an impulse thing.'

It was his gut talking. An instinct. He drove south towards California's ranch country and got a summer job baling hay. 'At night I could scarcely crawl into my bunk – absolutely dead to the world. But it sure toughened me up. It was about the happiest time of my life up till then. I had a couple of buddies at the time and we all set out to raise a little hell. It began with the cars.'

.   .   .

In a different era Clint Eastwood might have been a real cowboy and an adventurer. He was just a teenager when he started making money delivering newspapers and groceries. He might not have been a social whiz, but he was independent. It's the same today. He is more comfortable with his size ten Nike trainers up against the fire in the sunken patio of the Hog's Breath in Carmel than he is at the White House chatting with presidents and meeting Prince Charles and Princess Diana – at a 1986 dinner at which they all danced until 1:30 a.m. to an impromptu Neil Diamond 'concert'.

'I've worked ever since I was thirteen years old. My parents had a hard life when they were raising us. My father drilled into me that nobody does anything for you but yourself. Today we live in a welfare-orientated society and people expect more from Big Daddy government, more from Big Daddy charity. In my young days, that kind of society never existed. That philosophy never got you anywhere.

'I worked for every crust of bread I ever ate. Yet I always had a sense of future. I always had the feeling that discouraged as I was many times there was a place waiting for me at the top of the heap. I knew I had something to give. I don't think I had a colossal ego. Just the stupidity, perversity, premonition or whatever it is that gives a person a feeling of hope. That feeling of hanging in there.'

Eastwood had to hang in many times. He chanced death, courted disaster and became a real life hero before ever a camera rolled to the shout of 'Action'. But many times he felt a lost soul, just a man drifting along. His parents had continued to move around a lot and so, after leaving school, in an attempt to find some fixed point, he went to live with his grandmother for a time and raised chickens. 'I talked to chickens a lot' – in Hayward County on the outskirts of Oakland, California. He never didn't work but he couldn't settle. America was beginning to boom after the Second World War. The American Dream was the goal. What was happening to the schoolboy dreamer after he graduated from Oakland Public and Oakland Technical School in 1948 where he had been a more proficient basketball player than a scholar?

He was breaking his back digging ditches and swimming pools. Or working the midnight to 7 a.m. shift in front of a furnace at the Bethlehem Steelworks near Oakland. The sparks flew in the furnace. And when Eastwood and company went on the town. Says Roy Sturges who once worked alongside Eastwood at the furnace:

He was a man who worked real hard and paid himself by enjoying himself. We all believed we deserved a few beers and a good time after the hours we put in. And Clint wasn't one to hang back. He was a nice kid. Loyal. Always willing to help out if you had to go some place early or had a problem at home. He'd be the one to stand in for you. Always there.

Loyal. It's a word you hear much about Eastwood. He plays that role in the most extreme circumstances – and he expects it in return. It is part of the camaraderie he learned mucking in at the furnace or when digging ditches or waiting for the cry, 'Timber!' in the Oregon logging fields, when he was a tall, strapping lad and, like most teenagers, felt immortal. He soon learned that he wasn't.

Eastwood had always been fascinated by the logging business and managed to hire on in a mill operating on the Williamette River, near Eugene, Oregon. After only a few days on the job, he was nearly killed:

'I heard a shout and looked up and saw the crane driver and I hadn't quite got it organized. A nasty load of giant logs hung suspended over my head. I don't think I've reacted faster in my life. Yet even as I started to run, down came the logs. Any one of them could have crushed the life out of me. I just barely jumped clear – as the logs hit the ground they jammed against the crane which was a lucky break for me.

'The whole thing was. The money was good in the logging business and so was the food. The guys you met there were like wild characters out of a novel. It was pretty hard living but working outdoors in this fabulous country – rugged mountains, tall pine and fir forests – made it worth while. I never stayed long enough to work up into one of the really skilled jobs: if a man doesn't know what he's doing he can really pay for it. Some of the Douglas firs grew 250 to 300 feet tall and a man who goes up to the top of one of those to lop off the high branches has to be experienced. Log-rolling – that's riding the logs in mid-river – is another job where you either know what you're doing or you don't live long enough to have grandchildren. I earned good money felling trees. I'd pick where I wanted a tree to fall, take my axe and cut a 'V' so it would fall in that direction. Then another man and myself would work a two-man double saw. It took two of us because some of these trees were six feet in diameter. Some of the time was spent in the sawmill which was better pay but I preferred being outdoors.'

Today, Eugene, Oregon hasn't changed much since Eastwood's logging days except that it's a little quieter. He remembers: 'On weekends we all descended on Eugene and more or less turned the place inside out. Our manners weren't quite Ritz Hotel but the people in town were used to such behaviour from loggers. They were usually glad to see us. We were a lively bunch just out to whoop it up a bit. Most of the action was at a little place out of town where you could get a couple of beers and listen to some music. I've always preferred jazz, but I had fun listening to the badly played country-and-western stuff. It was so corny.

'Occasionally I'd talk to a girl. I can't say there was anything serious though. It was the wrong time for me. It wasn't that I was consciously steering clear of involvement, but I have this attitude towards responsibility – you don't undertake responsibilities until you are ready to handle them. I was earning good bachelor money but mentally I was still drifting. I had an idea I wasn't going to settle for tree-felling or sawmilling as my life's work but the way wasn't too clear.'

It soon became so. He had just turned twenty years old when the Korean War began on 25 June 1950. He knew he would be drafted, but 'I guess I was interested in living a little first,' he says now. And that meant San Francisco. He teamed up with several other footloose friends waiting to go into the army and they hit town. He's proud of the time they had: 'We enjoyed ourselves so much that by the time we reported for our physicals we were so exhausted and partied out that we thought we might fail our examinations. But we all made it.'

His love affair with Carmel was about to begin. And his infatuation with a girl that nearly cost him his life. Fort Ord is just another army camp – duty, discipline and dishwashing. Basic training was six weeks with no time off. But it was on the Monterey Peninsula and for that Eastwood will always be grateful. As he is that his father taught him to swim.

'I had an idea I might learn something while I was in the army and they had what were called Division Faculty Classes. I went to see the captain in charge and told him about the different jobs I had had since I left school. He asked me if I could swim. "Sure," I answered. He told me: "From this moment, Eastwood, you're assigned to the swimming pool. As an instructor." There was already a lieutenant and four sergeants running the pool so I can't say the work was too tough. Suddenly, everybody got shipped out to the front line – except me. I suppose my name just didn't come out of the hat. So there I was, a twenty-year-old private earning $76 a month in charge of an Olympic-size pool and organizing all the classes. It was a great opportunity. I moved out of the barracks and bedded down in one of the small dormitories attached to the pool. So long as I kept my nose clean and ran the place efficiently I was on my own. It was a real sweet set-up.

'Come 6 p.m. I'd knock off and go into Carmel and meet some girl. The money wasn't much so I decided to take a job at nights. Sure, buck privates weren't supposed to take civilian jobs in their spare time – but there wasn't anything in army regulations that said you couldn't. I signed up to work a swing shift with the Spreckles Sugar Company in the Salinas Valley. For four months when I'd finished my work at the pool, I'd shoot across to the Spreckles place and load sugar sacks or do maintenance work or anything they wanted. What I hadn't reckoned on was I'd need a little sleep now and then.

'After four months, I was the weariest swimming instructor in the army. I found myself falling asleep in the pool and drinking more water than was good for me. I figured I needed a change so I found a job in the junior non-commissioned officers' club. There were two other guys working there permanently, one behind the bar and the other on the floor to keep order, a bouncer. I quit the sugar factory and worked the NCO club which was only a minute's walk from the pool. It could be fairly wild in there. Maybe six or seven girls and 150 guys!

'The men weren't supposed to drink anything but beer which was free but a few of the smart guys would smuggle in some hard liquor and mix it in the beer. And that caused trouble. I had to bounce quite a few of them. Being big was a help.'

Eastwood never did get to Korea. But he nearly got killed anyway. For this time his size worked against him. He tells the story as though he was pitching a movie script. It's dramatic:

'It wasn't the girl's fault – she was real nice. I'd met her while visiting my folks in Seattle. I felt like seeing her again and mentioned it to a buddy who happened to be from Seattle. The problem was: how to get there and back on a weekend pass. Besides, there was the money involved.

'He said he could fix it. He explained that if you were in the service and in uniform, the naval air station at Monterey would fly you wherever you were going, if they had an extra seat on the aircraft. So I got a pass and headed out to Monterey. Sure enough, I found a little reconnaissance plane – going up to Seattle. Yes, there was room for me. So I flew up in style. I saw my mother and father and Jean. Then I went out with this very nice girl. I felt like I'd had a great weekend when I took off for the air base to hitch a ride back.

'There was nothing leaving for the south. I sat there, feeling dismal, trying to figure out what to do. The problem was: I had to fly back to get to camp in time – or I'd be AWOL. Dilemma: no money for a commercial air ticket. So I hung around asking every pilot in sight. Finally, I heard there was a naval torpedo bomber going to San Francisco. They didn't have any seats, of course.

'"Isn't there anywhere I could hang on?" I demanded desperately.

'"You could try the wings," said one of the pilots.

'He sized me up. "There's just one chance," he said. "But you're too big to squeeze into the radar compartment."

'I'd have turned myself into a midget at that moment, if necessary. But my legs alone looked as if they would fill the radar compartment. This was a little cubbyhole in the tail, with a tiny door, a little porthole and a big panel of instruments. Nobody was actually supposed to fly in there; the door was just for maintenance men to service the plane. But with a little shoving and pushing, they got me wedged in.

'Funny? Maybe. But it wasn't funny a little later. Everything that could go wrong with that trip went wrong. First of all, the compartment door sprang open and I nearly fell out – I guess my bulk was putting a little strain on it. So there I was, a mile or so up and no parachute and holding on for dear life.

'There was a little button you pushed to talk to the pilot, but the intercom wasn't working right and although I could hear him, he couldn't hear me. The pilot spotted the sprung door and warned me. He began shouting at me: "The door's open, soldier! Shut the door if you don't want to fall into the drink!" I kept yelling back at him, but he couldn't hear me. I can't say I was enjoying any of this – and even now, the thought is pretty grisly.

'Anyhow, I yanked out a cable, and got it looped round the handle of the sprung door; that kept it mostly shut. It still left a gap, however – and if you want to feel really miserable, I suggest you spend a couple of hours contemplating a nice long drop the way I did.

'Things got worse – fast! Before taking off, the pilot had warned me that he'd have to fly pretty high and I'd have to use the oxygen mask. As we climbed steadily, I put the mask to my face, only to discover it wasn't working. I fiddled desperately with it and tried to tell the pilot – but he still couldn't hear me. Last thing I remember before blacking out was him sending a message saying that although he could transmit, he couldn't pick up anything, but giving his position, estimated height and flying speed and adding that he had about two and a half hours fuel left – plenty to reach California.

'I remember nothing after that, except a kind of woozy, twilight feeling. Fortunately for me, the pilot's oxygen supply started going out, too, so he had to lose altitude. It must have been an hour later when I became aware of what was going on again and I realized that we'd hit California. It was easy to recognize, because the whole place was socked in by fog. I could hear the pilot talking again. He was telling the base he couldn't see anything, so he was going to hang out to sea a bit and see if he could get in under the clouds.

'Our danger now was that if we stayed over land, we might crash into a mountain; the pilot had to stay low because of his oxygen. I wasn't really worried yet; I had this feeling that if I'd got this far, I was going to survive. Then as we began circling round I remembered the fuel. I checked my watch and found it was about two and a half hours since the pilot had radioed that he had that much supply.

'I think I felt a little panic right then. I had no way of communicating with the pilot; I didn't know what kind of guy he was; would he eject and save himself by parachute and leave me and the plane to go down together? I knew he had the canopy above his head open, because the cable controlling it ran back through my compartment. But I couldn't figure I had much alternative except to hold on for dear life.

'The pilot must have spotted a hole in the clouds, because we dipped suddenly and went down fast. Next moment, through the porthole, I saw we were over the sea. I could see the whole coast of California now – beaches, cliffs and mountains, the tops of the latter invisible because of the fog. What I couldn't understand was why the pilot was flying over the water; why didn't he make straight for the city airport? Only later – much later – did I learn that the guy knew he was out of fuel and might crash on the city before making the airport. It was our lives against that of several hundred citizens. So there we wallowed, a few hundred feet above the sea, about a mile off the coast.

'And then the engine went – and it was a very deadening feeling, indeed. You could hear the air whistling – and I was watching the water and the beaches and cliffs and particularly the cables leading to the pilot's canopy; I sure wanted to know when he was going to leave the ship. I noticed he had the flaps down and realized he was going to come down in the water. I started wondering if the plane would float and began preparing for the moment we hit water, wedging myself in so that I would ride the shock.

'I saw the water was rough – it was going to be no easy landing. And then we were bouncing and bouncing – like a pebble skimming over water, and the ocean was just shooting in all over the place. You had the feeling that one moment you were in the air and next in a submarine. And then we stopped. We stopped with our nose down and our tail in the air. I found myself standing on the instrument board. I whipped off the cable holding the door and stepped out on to the back of the wings. The pilot was climbing out of his canopy and he leaped and landed beside me. He looked at me.

'Well, I hit the water and started to get out of there fast; I had an idea that if the plane started to sink, it would suck me down with it. So I just didn't hang around. It was sunset when we'd come down – and now the twilight was settling and it was getting dark. There was a big swell and very soon we were separated. We shouted a couple of times – but we were a long way from the beach and we needed every ounce of breath we had; so it became every man for himself.

'At certain times of the year, the Pacific gets full of phosphorous and you could tell where the beaches were because of the glow as the waves crashed on them. And then, almost the worst ordeal of all – I found myself in the middle of jelly fish! It was a creepy feeling. They were so close you could almost touch them, even see them in the phosphorous water. After all I'd been through, I didn't feel like being stung to death by jelly fish. I just clawed my way through.

'I don't know how long it took me to hit the beach, finally. But it was an ordeal I never want to go through again. When I was close to shore, I had to struggle desperately, because of the fierce undertow. Even when I was no more than twenty feet from the beach, I wasn't safe. I'd swim forward two feet and be carried back six. But inch by inch, I made it, until finally I felt bottom under my feet.

'I don't know how long I lay unconscious on the beach, but when I came to I was probably a little delirious. I vaguely remember running up and down the beach looking for the lieutenant, shouting his name until I was hoarse. I started imagining that every rock uncovered by the sea seemed to be his body – and I kept dashing back and forth in to the surf like a madman. For a time, I consoled myself with the thought that he'd probably come in a little distance away. Then, as I went several hundred yards in each direction, looking for him, I felt certain he had drowned, poor guy.

'I remember it was a peculiar contradictory feeling. I felt terribly depressed at this idea; yet strangely elated because it wasn't me. Anyhow, in the end, a little crazy by now, I guess, I began wandering off. I was barefoot – so I stayed at the water's edge rather than go inland. I went round some cliffs and there about eight miles in the distance I saw the lights of radio communications relay station.

'I don't remember anything, except that I looked at that light and kept walking towards it. Later, the guys at the RC station told me: "When you came through that door, buddy, you looked like a survivor of the Titanic."'

TWO

Shooting Star

'I sometimes think I've been working
all my life not to be famous – I don't
seem to have the gift it takes to enjoy
fame the way it should be enjoyed.'

CLINT EASTWOOD IN 1976

Eastwood was never again concerned about mortality, it was fate that dealt the cards. It was typical of him that he should survive on his own strength and merits. His image, his success, is all about the self-sufficient loner who can take care of himself and, if necessary, any trouble that happens. The code, the drive to his life is individuality and getting on with the job. Watch him on a film set and he'll be as likely as some casual worker to help move equipment or pour the coffee, a man in control of himself and the world around him.

That control is all important to him. And that includes the women around him. He talks of the 'strong' women of film that he admires, actresses like Barbara Stanwyck and Bette Davis, but this admiration has never carried over into his relationships. He's always been the Boss. He says his father told him: 'Nothing comes from nothing and don't plan on anything because no one gives you anything in life.' It's a cynical creed. But it is his appeal. People, audiences, want someone strong. They want to feel safe. They want assurance.

'Part of his sex appeal is the constant mystery – how deeply does he feel? How deeply is he involved in life?' says actress Susan Clark who co-starred with him in the 1968 *Coogan's Bluff*, the second movie in Don Siegel's rogue cop cycle about a country-boy cop taking on the big city as well as the bad guys.

His loose-limbed frame, the deep-set eyes and drawn cheeks on his parchment face – he can look ghostly in bad light – add to the enigmatic picture of him. And *nobody* knows quite what he's thinking. His longtime lover Sondra Locke would say: 'There's a certain distance, a certain mystery. He's always unapproachable to some degree.' But not if you're the right lady at the right moment. Fritz Manes is a stunt man and producer who knew Eastwood in the early days and offers:

Even in Junior High School, Clint was a solid loner – he didn't care for hanging out with the gang. He was always right on centre with himself, very sure of himself, so he didn't need the support of a circle of friends. Not that Clint ever lacked for companionship.

In high school he had a kind of natural charisma that was really maddening. You could sit in class and do all the little tricks of flirtation, flex your muscles, shuffle your $10 bills, and nothing would work if Clint was in the room. He'd be sitting there doing nothing, just looking at the floor and all the girls would be looking at him as if they were in a trance, locked in on some secret magnetism he had. It was very demoralizing for the rest of us guys.

During his spell in the army he met young actors David Janssen (who would star in television's *The Fugitive*) and Martin Milner (television's *Route 66*) and they kept saying Hollywood was also the place for him. He knew better. On the GI Bill he enrolled in a business course at Los Angeles City College.

The move was again motivated by a woman. Eastwood's friend Don Horner had a date with a girl from the University of California at Berkeley. Eastwood had what he recalls as 'tentative plans' with another girl. But Horner wanted to arrange a double-date and Eastwood went along. His blind date was Maggie Johnson, a five foot seven tall blonde – a true Californian girl in look and attitude. 'Maggie and I hit it off right away,' says the actor remembering: 'I can't say there was anything special about that night. I liked Maggie's sense of humour. I had no idea about marrying her.'

What happened was like the plot of one of those corny B picture romances they were churning out in the early fifties. He wasn't thinking marriage or commitment but this tall, suntanned and athletic girl graduated and was off south, home to Los Angeles. He decided to go too. While at college and living there, he helped pay the rent getting $30 a week for managing an apartment building in Beverley Hills. He worked at a garage in the evenings. At weekends he and Maggie went to the beach for barbecues, jazz and dancing, where they mixed with a young aspiring film crowd.

For those who lived in Los Angeles, the centre of the major film studios was a magnet. Many dreamed of showbusiness success.

'Clint was only twenty-three and so good looking I couldn't resist him,' Maggie Eastwood said of the long ago days. 'I was plain Maggie Johnson, a college student. We fell in love right away. We were married six months after we met.' That was on 19 December 1953 – Eastwood was on Christmas holiday from Los Angeles City College – and they went on honeymoon to – where else? – Carmel. They were married and living in a tiny, one-room apartment in downtown Los Angeles. He was studying. She was working in the office of a Los Angeles export business and doing some modelling.

It all changed suddenly: 'I remember him coming home one night all excited. He had met someone who wanted to give him a screen test.' Director Arthur Lubin had also offered tests to David Janssen and another aspiring actor hanging around the studios called Rock Hudson. Eastwood knows the story frame by frame:

'I'd met the director who was under contract to Universal Studios and he asked me: "Did they ever run a film test on you?" It had never occurred to me but I was definitely interested. I had nothing to lose but time. I went out to Universal the next week and it was fascinating. I'd never been in a film studio before. The director and the cameraman asked me if I'd ever done any acting – I told them about the school play. They decided to run a silent test on me to see how I photographed. I didn't feel I'd ever make it – it seemed like a little fun. There was no harm in it. They said they'd call me and I thought, Don't call us, we'll call you. But I was riding high and Maggie and I celebrated with dinner and a bottle of wine.'

It was seventeen days after his test that Universal Studios signed him to a contract.

.   .   .

His film career – at $75 a week – began with small parts in even smaller films like 1955's *Revenge of the Creature* and the talking-horse saga *Francis in the Navy* the same year. He lasted eighteen months at Universal – he and Burt Reynolds were fired on the same day by the same studio executive. Reynolds loves the story:

First he told Clint he had a chip on his tooth and said: 'You should get that fixed.' Clint never did. He also said: 'You speak too slowly – your Adam's apple sticks out too far.' When he turned to me I thought he was going to say my ears were too small or something wonderful. You know, I could make them bigger or something. Or put gum behind them and make them stick out. And he said: 'You have no talent.' So we got out. We were walking up the street and I turned to Clint and said: 'You know, I can learn to act. But you're going to have a hell of a time getting that Adam's apple out of your throat.'

But things weren't as much fun as the story. He did walk-on parts on television shows, some live TV work in New York and dug a lot of swimming pools back in Los Angeles. He was offered 1958's *Ambush at Cimarron Pass* which was to be a cheapie film in eight days. He calls it 'a Z movie, the lousiest Western ever made' but back then it was work. 'It was unbelievably bad and I said to myself: If you have to do more of this junk then quit.'

Westerns were the genre of the moment then on U.S. television: *Wagon Train* was an enormous success and the CBS television network wanted their own Western series. With this in mind, they commissioned *Rawhide* and Eastwood's agent, James Arthur, tried and tried to get him a shot on the series. He failed and failed. His wife encouraged him to keep going. And it was a friend of hers who accidentally got him his break. Maggie Eastwood's best friend, Sonie Chernus, was a story consultant at CBS. Eastwood went to visit and out of the door came Robert Sparks, a producer at the network. He stopped short and looked Eastwood up and down before hustling him into the office to meet Charles Marques Warren, the producer of *Rawhide*.

The late Eric Fleming had won the role of trail boss Gil Favor, but the network wanted another leading man on the show and had written Rowdy Yates, the ramrod or second-in-command of the trail herd. Eastwood – with Frankie Laine booming, 'Movin', movin', movin', keep these cattle movin', Rawhide!' – was boosted high up in the saddle for seven and a half profitable years coddling cattle in 254 episodes of the show. His work and play on the basketball court, in the swimming pool and the Oregon forests paid off. He did his own stunts. He looked like he was part of the horse. The series was a hit around the world. He was a television star – but not immediately.

'I made the pilot film and the first ten episodes and then nothing for six months. We had to wait until it was aired by CBS in order to see how the audience liked it and if we would continue. But the airing was postponed indefinitely. It didn't happen in September and by the terms of my contract, I couldn't see about other parts. Then in December, as we were about to take the train to San Francisco to spend Christmas with my folks, a telegram arrived. It said *Rawhide* had been scheduled as a mid-season replacement.' It began in January 1959.

Eastwood was cautious with his success and remembers his thoughts at the time: 'After a few years I would have liked to have done something else, but *Rawhide* was security. I remembered all those months without work and thought I'd ride it. Another disquieting thought was that few big television personalities ever transferred successfully to theatrical films. 'What hope did I have?'

He wasn't so cautious about romance. Incredibly, he has pursued a career in one of the most public of arenas but his secret life has only now become public. The way Maggie Eastwood talks, it is as if they had an open marriage for many years. Certainly, people who have worked with Eastwood on his films have talked about how brazenly he has pursued the ladies. And not just to flirt but in a serious way. There was a lot of talk about his extra-marital love life – talk that didn't get into the Hollywood gossip columns. A crew member who worked on one of his films said: 'Clint goes where he wants, does what he wants – goes to dinner with a girl if he wants. Maggie doesn't say a word. Clint is the undisputed boss.'

Eastwood was asked about this and responded at the time: 'Maggie doesn't chain me down. The worst thing is owning people. I don't want to be owned by anybody – maybe shared, but not owned, lock, stock and barrel. Like: "Where were you?" or: "Who's that?" That's like two attorneys battling – the beginning of the end. It kills more relationships than anything – clutch, grab, lust. Squelches the spirit. To me love for a person is respect for individual feelings. Love is respecting privacy, accepting faults.

'But don't believe it's a one-way street. The sophisticated woman accepts that chances are a guy's not being 100 per cent faithful. If she talks about it, it only makes it worse; best way to get a guy to be unfaithful is to talk about it. The beginning is infatuation – after that it becomes other things. Love isn't across a room: it is a long time. Sex is a small part of life – 99.9 per cent of your life is spent doing other things. And if you accept a guy, you have to make that guy feel important so he gets satisfaction. It's selfish – you give love to get love. Women have the toughest roles – it's easier to be on the offensive than the defensive.'

Eastwood and Maggie, who was also his career mentor pushing him forward for roles and advising him on scripts, waited fifteen years after their December 1953 marriage before their son, Kyle, was born. When he's asked about it he shoots off: 'Planned parenthood,' but people close to the couple in those days believe that Maggie Eastwood had to fight to have her first child. Maggie herself says: 'Clint and I were both "moving" people and we didn't think we could manage in a one-room apartment. We decided we wouldn't have kids until we could afford help.' Kyle Eastwood was born in 1968.

Clint Eastwood's illegitimate daughter was born four years earlier on 17 June 1964, at Cedars of Lebanon Hospital in Los Angeles. It was a secret for more than a quarter of a century. *Rawhide* was a success in 1959 when Eastwood first met Roxanne Tunis who was then twenty-eight years old and a stunning, tall and attractive brunette. He was the star. She was a sometime screen extra, stunt woman and occasional actress. According to those who worked on the series, Roxanne Tunis was no starry-eyed fan. Like so many, she was overwhelmed by the Eastwood charm. They acted like a couple on the set of the series while his wife Maggie was back at home in Carmel.

With Eastwood's help, Roxanne found more success as an actress – and became pregnant. He will not talk about it, so we can only imagine the dilemma. He was a star and he was married, and in 1964 the term 'love child' had not even been used. There was potential for scandal and he was still working at establishing his career, but he was pragmatic – and so was Roxanne. She would have the child but in secret and he would support them for the rest of their lives. There would be no gossip. They have both kept to their bargain.

Kimber Tunis has her father's face and there is also a family resemblance in her son – Eastwood's grandson – Clinton Eastwood Gaddie who was born on 21 February 1984, in Oxnard, California. Kimber moved from Los Angeles to Denver, Colorado with her mother in 1974. Her son is from her 1983 marriage to gardener and tree specialist, Anthony Gaddie. They are now divorced. Eastwood provided funds for schooling and holidays and treats for Kimber as well as buying their home in Denver. They were all sworn to a secrecy pact but when Kimber grew up and had a child of her own she would say:

I don't make any decisions without him. He makes the decisions about every part of our lives. He loves his grandson and sees him when he can. I don't know what he will feel about this becoming public.

Later he reacted typically and his way of controlling the situation was to turn his back completely on his illegitimate daughter and first grandson.

Maggie Eastwood knew about the other family and even met Roxanne on the set of the film *Breezy* which her husband was directing in 1972. Eastwood went white – he was totally shaken – when Maggie arrived with their son Kyle and confronted Roxanne. But the two women had a 'civilized' meeting and Roxanne played with Kyle while Eastwood shied away supposedly concerned about a camera set-up with his star William Holden. It was an intriguing time in Eastwood's love life. That year he had also met Sondra Locke who had auditioned for a role in *Breezy*, a role which Eastwood would decide was not for her. But he remembered her later.

The former Mrs Eastwood will not be drawn into discussions about meeting Roxanne, just as she will say 'no comment' when asked about her feelings towards Sondra Locke. But she does tell us enough to see what was going on in Eastwood's life – a busy one socially as well as professionally – at the time he first became involved with Roxanne.

With Rawhide *everything changed. Before we knew it we had some money, a house with a pool and were forever posing for pictures as Hollywood's latest young and exciting couple. It was new to us so we didn't mind all the publicity and the pictures. We didn't live the Hollywood life, but we went to some parties. The glamour and the glitter weren't our whole life. In Hollywood people said we had a perfect marriage. Well, it wasn't always perfect. No marriage ever is. In a way, the end of our marriage was inevitable.*

Other women? I was never realistic about some things. I used to always hope for the best. I wanted to protect myself. I wondered about it but I didn't dwell on it because it would probably have driven me insane. I just preferred to hang in there and not to worry too much about it.

While Maggie Eastwood kept her private feelings somewhat concealed, professionally, it was Eastwood who was feeling frustrated. He had been hunky Rowdy Yates for seven years – and how long can you take Frankie Laine booming in your ears? When *Rawhide* had begun on American television, there were forty other Western series in competition on screen. As the years went on, Eastwood learned about film editing, how each show was pieced together, and he asked if he could film scenes himself from horseback. Then, he asked to direct an episode. The producers had enough evidence of stars messing up to say no. He had watched James Garner move from *Maverick* on television to the big screen and seen Steve McQueen vault from *Wanted Dead or Alive* to becoming one of the top five movie stars in the world.

Eastwood was fed up enough reluctantly to accept – after James Coburn had rejected the offer – the lead in a film which had the prophetic title *A Fistful of Dollars*. Much has been written about the minimalism of the film. It has been the basis of scholarly thought. What it meant. Who Eastwood's character the Man with No Name was. In reality, it was a low-budget Western being made for $200,000 in Spain by a non-English speaking Italian director called Sergio Leone. In 1964 no one was offering Eastwood anything else in the movies. And all involved got lucky.

What was to change Eastwood's life and some aspects of movie-making was his own style and gut instincts. Leone, who died in 1991, had made sword and sandals movies like *Sodom and Gomorrah* and this was a similar exercise. At first, Eastwood reckoned that the less his character talked, the more mystique. But he doesn't take the credit: 'It was all there in the script. Even *Yojimbo*, the Samurai picture it was taken from, was the same. Yeah, a little broadness but I'd been doing 200 *Rawhides* and I was ready for anything different in doing a Western. The Western in

America had reached a real dead period as far as imagination was concerned.'

But Eastwood almost didn't become 'Il Cigaro' to the Italians, 'El Cigarillo' to the Spanish or 'Herr Wunderbar' to the Germans and box-office magic world-wide to audiences who hung on his every silence. Eastwood recalls his first days in Spain:

'I scuffed around in the dirt all morning waiting for the director and the crew to quit arguing. The talk was all in Spanish and Italian and I didn't understand a word but I could tell there was a violent discussion going on about something. I hoped they'd get it straightened out before we blew the whole morning without getting one shot. Finally, Sergio called me over.

'"OK, Clint, you can start making up," he said through his interpreter. What the heck, I decided – they were always at it. Trouble was this outfit didn't have much money so there was always arguments about paying the crew. But then I wouldn't have been in Spain if they had a lot of money – they'd have gone for James Stewart or Bob Mitchum if they'd been loaded. So I figured I'd put up with some disorganization.

'Making-up was a nice, slow job if you didn't mind the sticky heat and the flies and the dust. The scene called for a lot of make-up because my face was to be badly swollen from being beaten up by a whole gang. I came out from under the job feeling hot and uncomfortable and headed for the set. I was literally the most alone man in Spain. The set was deserted. No producer, no director, no crew. Only the big arc lamps standing there like Spanish vultures. It seems the crew hadn't been paid for two weeks and they had left the set until someone came through with their money. This wasn't the first time this had happened. It was just one foul-up after another. But this time, with one eye sealed shut by make up and all the other junk on my face, I'd had it.

'Maybe I hurt too easily inside. I used to flare up at the drop of a hat until I learned better. I made a decision – I told them they could find me at the airport. Fortunately, Sergio caught me before I left the hotel. He apologized and promised it wouldn't happen again. Things ran a little smoother after that, but they were far from perfect, but we got through the film.'

Maggie Eastwood remembers:

He was paid $15,000 for that. Suddenly, we heard the critics in Europe loved the film. That's when I knew Clint was going to be a big star. Well, for years I was the Woman With No Name. I was this big Hollywood star's wife, yet I never had an identity of my own. He had this thing about being a loner, like I didn't exist at times. He's a very complex person.

Buoyant and burly Sergio Leone would not have used the word 'complex' about his American star. He found him 'strange' and not at all what he expected when their partnership began. Eastwood was changing the rules: 'I always was a different kind of person even when I started acting,' says the actor following with the wonderful admission: 'I guess I finally got to a point where I had enough nerve to do nothing. My first film with Leone had a script with tons of dialogue, tremendously expository, and I just cut it all down. Leone thought I was crazy. Italians are used to much more vocalizing and I was playing this guy who didn't say much of anything. I cut it all down. Leone didn't speak any English so he didn't know what the hell I was doing but he got so he liked it after a while . . .

'The original screenplay had endless pages of dialogue all explaining the character's background but I wanted to play it with an economy of words and create this whole feeling through attitude and movement. It was just the kind of character I had envisioned for a long time – keep to the mystery and allude to what happened in the past. It came about after the frustration of doing *Rawhide* for so long. I felt the less he said the stronger he became and the more he grew in the imagination of the audience. You never knew who he was, where he came from and what he was going to do next.

'I had spent many years playing the sort of Mr Good Guy. There was something I liked about going against every Western tradition. Usually, no one played the protagonist where he enters town and sees a woman and child crying for help and essentially rides on. But that gives him somewhere to go during the movie. He can become interested in the parties against his will. The producers thought something was really awry. "Hey, this guy isn't doing anything – he doesn't even have a name." But when they saw it assembled and how it went over with the public, they realized what it was. The "No Name" guy soon became a very imitated character.'

'Eastwood *was* the character,' said Leone recalling the early days of the partnership in the American film magazine *Film Comment* in 1978. A decade later he admitted in a conversation in Beverley Hills that he had felt intimidated by Eastwood – but it didn't stop him cashing in on the cult he had created with his star. After *A Fistful of Dollars* (originally entitled *The Magnificent Stranger*) in 1964 came *For a Few Dollars More* in 1965 and *The Good, the Bad and the Ugly* in 1966. For whatever reason, and it would seem to be more happenstance and the circumstances of the sixties than some cleverly thought-out promotion, Eastwood rode off on a mule at the end of *A Fistful of Dollars* and into the sunset and cult status. The poncho. The badly chewed cigars – non-smoker Eastwood recalls: 'If I had to be in an unpleasant frame of mind, I took a couple of draws and, boy, I was right there' – and the squint and fast draw compromised the picture of the grizzled gunslinger, the anti-hero, the Man With No Dialogue as well as no name. It was of the times. In the upheaval of sixties Britain Michael Caine had just created Len Deighton's working-class hero from *The Ipcress Files* on screen in 1965, and that womanizing bounder *Alfie* in 1966. In America, entering equally turbulent times,

Eastwood was the icy-eyed con of the age of Vietnam, 'Clint is the quintessential Western man,' says Susan Clark adding: 'He has a certain code and he adheres to it religiously.'

After working with him, the late Richard Burton said his co-star in *Where Eagles Dare* had 'dynamic lethargy'. You could also get away with that description for Lee Van Cleef who was another American actor imported by Sergio Leone for his Westerns. Van Cleef believes *For a Few Dollars More* is the best of the Eastwood/Leone partnership. In an interview before his death he told me: 'It had more depth to it. There was more subtlety about the film and about the performance. And Clint had the confidence then. He had the character down. He's playing it minimal and it worked.'

Van Cleef went along with Eastwood and Eli Wallach in *The Good, the Bad and the Ugly* in the search for hidden gold and said: 'We had a good time. Clint was really easy to work with. He was professional. And while it was clear he had that star quality, it didn't make him anything other than one of the guys.'

The actor who played bad guys for most of his career knew a lot about his stars. He played on the spaghetti and paella train in Italy and Spain for several years after Eastwood returned to mainstream American movies:

> *I think Clint's timing was good. He was fresh then, a new face for the movies and he had the experience from all those years on* Rawhide *and working with Leone. I knew when I worked with him that it was just a matter of time. He always had control of the situation. There were all those guys babbling away – at times we couldn't understand them and at times they didn't have a clue what we were saying. But, somehow, it all worked. And then when the movies were seen outside Europe there was no stopping.*

A Japanese film critic put the tamp on the legend when he called the trio of Eastwood films 'macaroni Westerns'. One man's pasta became another man's spaghetti, but it wasn't suddenly all champagne life – or a very public one. In the sixties he had been happy to pose with Maggie by their swimming pool, learning his lines, having her trim his hair and other excuses for different sorts of publicity pictures to promote *Rawhide*. But, after filming *The Good, the Bad and the Ugly*, he returned to California with a completely different attitude. He wanted control. Total control of his career and of his marriage. Hollywood thought he had got lucky in Europe. 'Just fluke hits,' they said. He says his thoughts then were: 'I was appalled not only at the way money was misused but also the lack of control that an actor had over characters.'

The Italian producers of the spaghetti Westerns had not envisioned how much of a box-office superman their nihilistic hero was to become and had not arranged all world copyrights. When they were legally able to release the Leone films in the United States, Eastwood hit American cinemas with a one, two, three punch and scored a knockout every time as the three movies were shown in the one year – 1967. And he kept up the pressure by starring that year in Ted Post's *Hang 'Em High* which might have been made-in-the-USA but for its very Leone pasta flavour. The movie did wonderful business returning costs in ten weeks, the fastest turnaround in the history of the United Artists Studios.

Still much more fun and well received was *Coogan's Bluff*, which gave us Eastwood as a hayseed Old West lawman going against the odds in the big city. The film, the basis of the television series *McCloud* which starred Dennis Weaver, was made the same year as *Hang 'Em High* and was to begin Eastwood's high energy work pattern. The critics liked *Coogan's Bluff*. Still, they were not convinced about the star. He was.

Eastwood completed *Coogan's Bluff* for Universal Studios on New Year's Eve 1967. He flew to London the same day and reported for work on *Where Eagles Dare* on 2 January 1968. He was being paid $750,000 and getting the same billing as Burton who was then an acting and marital legend. It didn't bother Eastwood – the man with all that 'dynamic lethargy' – one bit. 'People recognize me wherever I go and like it. But that's just part of success.'

The other part was control and clout. And the luxury of having his views about violence and sex listened to. On violence he offered: 'I am not an advocate of violence, but on the other hand, if it is one of the narrative elements in the story, I am not as upset by it as other people are. The world is a violent place – no one can escape that. In films, when it is justified, violence acts as a sort of release. Sex? It's used to stimulate and probably some people wish they were involved and in the same situation they are looking at, but sex in the movies is not the type of animal release violence is, although sometimes it is intended that way. When I'm working, I like to use my imagination.'

He needed it after agreeing to star in his first musical, the $20 million budgeted *Paint Your Wagon*. The director, Josh Logan, was delighted to get Eastwood in 1969 saying:

Fortunately, this is the year of Clint Eastwood. We were looking for a man who could be a leading man and a romantic threat to Lee Marvin's love for Jean Seberg – he's strong physically and as a personality.

Yet, when Logan's prized star turned up for the first day of filming *Paint Your Wagon* – driving his pick-up truck – the studio guard refused to let him in. 'What did I do? I turned around and went back to my office and got on with some work. Then the calls began coming in. I may say I took my time about getting back.' Considering the film's poor critical and box-office reception, it might have been better if he'd been kept out. Along with the rest of the cast including affable but vodka-prone Marvin and the fragile and beautiful actress Jean Seberg, both of whom are now dead.

Seberg always wanted real men. Eastwood personified her desires. And was willing to go along with them. Those who were on the location in Oregon support longtime rumours that Eastwood and Seberg had a passionate affair during the making of the film. Eastwood himself has never acknowledged the affair. Or denied it.

He was quizzed about his marriage between the time of filming *Paint Your Wagon* and *Two Mules for Sister Sara* which found him down in the Mexican jungle. The actress Susan St James was with him but not exclusively. There was another never identified date. 'Maggie doesn't chain me,' was Eastwood's repeated reaction back then to the tales of the many ladies in his life, while Maggie Eastwood was back in Carmel, swimming, or playing tennis, entertaining herself. And he expanded in 1969: 'When I finish a film I drift back to my own little area where I can be with people I want to and ten minutes later with no one. I'm really all about Carmel, off-in-the-backwoods stuff. If I get really uptight, I go up alone or my wife will go ahead of me. Most of the time I'm off with a flick – I bounce back and forth. She usually comes to every location after I'm situated, visits awhile, and then leaves. She's travelled all over the world, has demands at home. Selfishly, I like things organized.'

As another fast-gun drifter in *Two Mules for Sister Sara* he rescues co-star Shirley MacLaine's nun Sara from three rapists. Sara, a prostitute disguised as a nun, then goes on a trek with her protector across Mexico until they take on a French garrison. Years later, Eastwood still gets enthusiastic about the film which was directed by his friend and mentor Don Siegel: 'Westerns are designed as men's shows. I haven't worked with many actresses who have been turkeys. Once in a while you'd get a stiff who'd be looking in at the make-up table all the time.'

On location, back then, he was asked point blank: 'Are you happy?'

The question was centred not on his career but his private life and he replied: 'Either happy or extremely loyal.' Complex, said Maggie Eastwood. Strange, said Sergio Leone. Also troubled? Certainly, confident. And easily bored. '*Paint Your Wagon* took six months to make – it should have been three. It made me crazy, all that hanging around. *Where Eagles Dare* took five months. A monumental bore. I hated seeing money flung away like that. So I decided it was time to make my own pictures. If studios want to chuck their money away that's up to them. I want no part of it.' Eastwood was about to make the move which makes him today the richest movie star in the world.

THREE

Top Gun

'My dad was Scots-English, my mother Dutch-Irish, strange combinations. All the pirates and people who were kicked out of everywhere else.'

CLINT EASTWOOD IN 1983

Eastwood's reaction to his experience and frustration with the film world was to go into business for himself. 'My theory was that I could foul up my own career just as well as anybody else so why not try it?' It was 1968 and he was still fussed over by a business adviser who had told him going to Spain to make *A Fistful of Dollars* was a 'bad step'. He formed the Malpaso Company which is named after a creek that runs through the Monterey Peninsula. It is also – Eastwood tells you with a smile – Spanish for 'bad step'. Beginning as a small bungalow at the Burbank Studios in Hollywood, today, in 1992, it is still there as the centre of Eastwood's company, known as the Taco Bell because it so resembles a chain of rough and ready Mexican fast-food restaurants of that name. In the sixties Eastwood was happy working there with a few cans of beer, a couple of pencils, a few pieces of paper and was equally frugal about personnel. Already a major star, he had a staff of four. The Doris Day television series in production at the same time had a staff of twenty-six.

'All you need to get into the Directors' Guild of America is for someone to give you a job. So I gave myself a job. I said: "Kid, you got a job."' Maggie Eastwood was up in Carmel with Kyle and her husband commuted up the Pacific Coast Highway. Or maybe stayed at the office. He was preparing for the first film for Malpaso entitled *The Beguiled* and directed by Don Siegel. It was to be audiences' first glimpse into Eastwood's personal fascination with sex and violence, of lust over innocence. He played a soldier during the American Civil War who hides out in a girls' school like a boy in a sweetshop. Immediately, he starts flirting with the students. In return for his attention they start to poison him. Then, they cut off his leg.

More significant was *Play Misty for Me* in 1971 which was Eastwood's début as a director. He revealed in 1991 that the film is based on a real story of sexual harassment. And it was Eastwood who was harassed. He says he was nineteen and the girl was around twenty-three and quietly comments: 'There was a little misinterpretation about how serious the whole thing was.' He used his own experience and that of a disc jockey in California's Mendocino County to create his character in *Play Misty for Me*, which more than twenty years later remains a highly regarded cult film. Jessica Walter had the best part as the demented fan stalking disc jockey Eastwood and his screen girlfriend, which gave Donna Mills her breakthrough role. Now immensely popular as Abby on the long-running American soap *Knot's Landing*, Donna Mills was then very much a newcomer to Hollywood.

I had done some guest shots on television including Burt Reynolds' show Dan August. *Apparently, Burt and Clint were talking and Clint had tested 300 girls for the role of the girlfriend, which is a lot of auditions. Burt told him to watch my part on* Dan August. *Clint went in and saw a rough-cut [an un-edited version] of the show and said: 'That's the girl.' He hired me right from it. I was on a soap in New York and I never met him until I came out to Hollywood – it all happened that fast. It was the first time he had directed and it was wonderful. He really was wonderful. He knew exactly what he wanted. We shot the film in six weeks which is not a long time for a major feature.*

I liked him a lot, but he was married and we were very proper. I have always made it a rule of my life that I never go out with married men – no matter how attracted I am to them or how appealing they are. I think it's a real heartache for everybody involved.

She did have one refreshing love scene with her co-star – under a freezing cold waterfall. 'Clint brought out a bottle of cognac to warm us up – by the time we both got through the scene we were bombed. Clint and I became very good friends after the movie and stayed in touch a long while.'

And he had made another point to the Hollywood executives who questioned his decision to give Jessica Walter the grand standing psycho role. 'The studio people said why do you want to do a movie where the woman has the best part? My reaction was Why not? I figured, why should men have all the fun playing disturbed characters? If you think about it the best characters – the roles with a little conflict and zip to them – are the villains.'

Unless they're *Dirty Harry*. Inspector Harry Callahan was the Man With No Name but in a neatly cut suit, clean shave and shirt and conservative tie. And he had the big .44 Magnum gun which liberals dubbed as 'an angry erection' and legendary *New Yorker* critic Pauline Kael termed 'fascist medievalism'. Of course, in 1971 it was an instant hit, as a fast-moving film directed by Siegel who was by now Eastwood's unofficial partner. Harry was the great cop who was stopped from catching his man – a sex killer played by Andy Robinson – by bureaucracy, by the system. The blue-collar appeal was instant – here was another anti-hero but this time trying to do everything possible to clean-up the streets. D.H. Lawrence had observed years earlier: 'The essential American soul is hard, stoic, isolate and a killer.' And *Dirty Harry* translated that thought of the literary man to the man-in-the-streets world-wide. But in the Vietnam era the controversy was fierce. When the Philippines announced they were using *Dirty Harry* as a police training film, there were howls of derision.

The advertisement for the movie ran: 'You Didn't Assign Dirty Harry – You Turned Him Loose' and Eastwood would never be drawn into the political debate that went on around it. But he did have answers about the violence: 'Violence is a fact of life. It's what people are most curious about – like slowing down to see car crashes on the highway. It's unusual. It goes on the front pages of newspapers, not the back page. That's what people want to know about. What about people who don't accept that? I tell them to fuck off.'

He's adamant: 'A lot of people thought it was a political film and it wasn't at all. He's just an individual who has a certain philosophy about victims of crime. But that story was a bit ahead of its time. Nowadays, there's organizations for victims of violent crimes and for the families but in those days there wasn't any of that. I don't necessarily agree with Dirty Harry's philosophy all the way down the line. I don't disagree with the importance of rights for the accused either. But we were telling a story. Dirty Harry was just a person who had questions about the law – I don't think there is a person in America who isn't frustrated by a lot of our court decisions.' Eastwood's uncanny instincts were proven accurate when the worst urban violence ever in the United States forced President George Bush to send in the National Guard and the army to take back control of the looted and burning streets of Los Angeles in the late spring of 1992. It wasn't only Los Angeles which turned into an inferno following the acquittal of four LA police department officers in the beating of black motorist Rodney King. There were demonstrations and riots across America, including Eastwood's home town of San Francisco.

In 1971 the *Dirty Harry* scenes the fans adored and most imitated were the most loathed by the civil rights groups. Especially the scene where Harry is pointing his big gun at the wounded bank robber he is standing over:

> *I know what you're thinking. Did he fire six bullets or only five? Well, to tell the truth, I kinda lost track myself. But seein' how the .44 Magnum is the most powerful handgun in the world and that it would blow your head clear off, you got to ask yourself – Do I feel lucky today? Well, do ya punk?*

At that moment Harry pulls the trigger and it clicks on an empty chamber. The punk is messing himself. Harry flashes his roguish grin.

Americans called him a fascist. French film buffs already were rating him an *auteur*. Audiences were turning out for everything he did. With *Play Misty for Me* – the *Fatal Attraction* of its day just as 1984's *Tightrope* preceded the 1992 sex and cops chiller

Basic Instinct – and *Dirty Harry* the same year, 1971, he was on his way as the biggest box-office star of the seventies. And to meet Sondra Locke who would end his marriage at a cost to him of more than $20 million. And who would later shatter his faith in 'the loyalty of friends'.

Throughout their long relationship, Locke, who married sculptor Gordon Anderson in 1967, remained married. And in 1992 still is. And it still is bizarre. As extraordinary as his marriage was. As Maggie Eastwood has said, the end of her marriage was inevitable. What was extraordinary was how long it stayed to-gether, at least officially, given the private pressures and extra-marital relationships involved.

But worker Eastwood was still pursuing his other passion of film-making, oblivious to his complex private life. In 1972 he made the Western *Joe Kidd* on location in Arizona. It was familiar territory. Just a bigger star role. Eastwood was the gunfighter protecting Mexican workers against monied interests. He also had to protect himself against the ladies, one of whom, ever forward, approached him in the film's location hotel and asked: 'What does it take to stay the night with you?'

'A lot of things crossed my mind, but I just laughed and scratched my way out of the problem.'

The movie-making continued as in 1973 Eastwood directed the love story *Breezy* which starred William Holden. He was casting the film and interviewed Sondra Locke who had won an Oscar nomination for her first film *The Heart is a Lonely Hunter* in 1968. She was twenty-one then and played a fourteen year old in the much admired screen adaptation of Carson McCullers's novel. She desperately wanted the role especially with Holden leading the cast. She didn't get it. But the producer and director of the film would recall her later.

Inspector Harry Callahan returned in 1973 in *Magnum Force* to more outcry and in 1974 Eastwood co-starred in the buddy picture *Thunderbolt and Lightfoot* directed by Michael Cimino with the young Jeff Bridges. Eastwood was on the list of the Top Ten box-office stars with John Wayne and Paul Newman from 1969 and by 1975 he was top of the heap – literally. *The Eiger Sanction* was a slight international espionage story but the thrills were in the mountaineering stunts. Eastwood did his own. And nearly got himself killed while only rehearsing for Swiss location scenes. He took on rock faces at California's Yosemite National Park. With him was cinematographer-mountaineer Mike Hoover who watched as Eastwood 'flamed-out' from the rock face and was dangling in space unable to get to safety. Hoover remembers how:

He looked at me and said: 'Gee, I don't think I can make it.' I said, 'Well, Clint, you really don't have much choice, do you?' Then he reacted characteristically – he got pissed off. He pulled in his chin, he gritted his teeth and with absolutely no technique at all, just blood and guts, he moosed his way up. No skill, no brains, just pure muscle. It was gruesome to watch.

Much more gruesome was the filming on the Eiger when a British climber and stunt man was killed, and Hoover himself narrowly escaped death. David Knowles who was twenty-seven when the film was being made in 1975, was from Preston, Lancashire. Eastwood was hanging from a rock face a few yards from Knowles who was hit by a falling boulder and killed, while Hoover who was struck by the rock had his pelvis fractured.

Filming went on and all the climber stunt men accepted the accident for what it was. 'They are a breed apart – they strike up a great camaraderie between themselves,' recalled Eastwood. Hoover remembered it differently:

He always comes off as very callous and pragmatic but inside he's mush. He was shaken by the accident – he even started to cry. And he was ready to shut down production of the film. He's the first guy to do the dirtiest job – and not in a show-off way. Clint seemed so simple I thought he was phoney, but after a while I realized how sharp he was. He isn't verbal, but he's one smart mother.

Which is why after making *The Eiger Sanction*, Eastwood said: 'I will never do anything like that again – just too damn dangerous. Even though I had practised for weeks, it was still terrifying. I don't see how you can ever get used to dangling on the end of a rope, thousands of feet above nothing, held up by a man you hardly know. And when a glacier moves with that terrible groan, that's terrifying. One of the British guys said I'd get used to it. I never did.'

Professionally, Eastwood has always been surefooted – none of those bad steps – sometimes a difficult hurdle but nothing dramatically wrong. But he was struggling to reach firmer ground with his family – now including a daughter, Alison, who was born in 1973 – when smack in the middle of the seventies he began pre-production thinking about 1976's *The Outlaw Josey Wales*, one of his classic films. The plot has emotional twists with his own life at that time. Josey Wales loses his family to a band of guerrillas during the Civil War. He goes after the bad guys. Then a crazy Yankee captain slaughters surrendering rebel troops. Josey survives and picks up an odd-ball team of pilgrims on his travels as he seeks revenge: a dying frontier boy played by Sam Bottoms, an old Indian with some of the film's best lines portrayed by Chief Dan George and a lost young woman – Sondra Locke.

Locke is a wisp of a thing. Blonde and fragile. American. Deep South born. Which in *The Outlaw Josey Wales* was fine – on the surface. She had attended a 'cattle call' – an audition of more than 2000 actresses – to win her part in *The Heart is a Lonely Hunter* but was concerned at her success in it: 'I was afraid it had put me into some kind of sexual oblivion. I played a practically pre-puberty tomboy and some producers thought I was a boy.'

Eastwood changed the image. In *The Gauntlet*, which followed *Josey Wales* in 1977 and mirrors its humour, he has her in skin-tight jeans and an open top taunting a bunch of bad boy bikers: 'Let's see what you've got between your legs.' In the film she's a very tough good-time girl helping Eastwood's hard-drinking Arizona cop. But it was from the Western *Josey Wales* that they became something of a contemporary Spencer Tracy and Katherine Hepburn. They made love together. They made films together. Polite people only discussed the films. It was a long relationship – a major commitment by so high profile a star as Eastwood. Maggie Eastwood did what was required and that was to support her husband in all his endeavours. It could not have been easy.

Eastwood and Locke sparkled on screen. Off screen they did too. During filming of *The Gauntlet* the battle-of-the-sexes sparring sometimes overflowed off screen. Locke appeared with Eastwood in six films including the *Dirty Harry* excursion *Sudden Impact* in 1983. She says they had lived together as man and wife from 1977. In an exclusive interview at the Bel-Air Hotel in Los Angeles, she talked about their lives together in great detail. She is less forthcoming about their lives apart now that many of the court papers have been made secret by the Los Angeles Superior Court.

She always felt lucky in their relationship. People talked. It was part of the territory. She accepted the strange set-up. She was married. He was married. They were a couple. When you listen to her talk about her life before and then with Eastwood you get an understanding of the man and woman who were Hollywood's Odd Couple for so long.

The only way to get a rest is just to leave Los Angeles – to get out of town. To get away from business is the only way to relax. I've always done that. We did that.

Some friends of mine have some places up in Oregon and in Northern California and Idaho and it's such beautiful country I take off there and collapse. I read and walk. And you know it's amazing. I find everybody asks me what do you do, don't you get bored? I find that when I get in the country I don't know what it is but I find there's never enough time in the day, the day goes by so fast and I'll think: Oh, I wanted to write such and such a letter today or I something else. Well, there's no time. I suppose the smallest task seems a monumental thing at the end of the day. I go with friends but away from business and away from Hollywood, and the telephone.

Quite frankly, any career I've had is because it just came to me because I am the worst at producing a career. It just is totally against my grain. I don't like going to places where I don't know people, I don't like new people. It's a terrible thing to say and it has to do with Hollywood. That sounds a cliché in a way but it's basically true. I'm just no good at pushing my own career. Period. So it's amazing that I've had one at all.

I've worked in a lot of Clint's pictures but I've never got into the celebrity circuit. I think that he's the same way too in that respect. He keeps himself outside of the Hollywood scheme of things. But basically I'm so bad at that. I love to work. I really love acting. I love the film process. I love the set. I'm interested in all aspects of film making.

I really love movies, ever since I was a child, but I am so bad at business. Agents or managers don't really do anything that much for you. They're very good at negotiating if someone wants you and once in a while an agent probably has done a lot for a client, got them started or pushed them hard but in the general sense, I think it comes down to the person. You have to get out there and you have to make the contacts and you have to be seen, you have to know this person, that person, you have to make yourself available. Out of sight, out of mind.

I've never done that and it's not that I don't care about my career and that I don't want to work, because I've been

50

disappointed that there aren't enough roles that I was sad that I didn't get. There isn't a lot to get you excited most of the time, but there have been a few things, you know. I think working once a year would be ideal really! An actor can make one really good film a year, that's accomplishment because there isn't that much great material.

I really don't mind leisure time. Even if I were getting offers right and left, I'm not the person who wants to work all the time. I'm compulsive in accomplishing projects, but I don't always have to be focused on something, it doesn't have to be movies or working . . . I always think, Oh, I'll never work again. I think actors, no matter how successful they are, always think that, Oh, this is the last one, I'll never work again. I can remember when I did *The Heart is a Lonely Hunter* with Alan Arkin and he said that. And at that time Alan was very hot, everyone was interested in him. I remember thinking to myself, Oh, this is incredible, all this.

But I got that part just as part of the process of a talent search because I was right out of high school. I had never done anything except local theatre and I was very interested in it and I auditioned. That's the only time I've ever pursued acting in my life. I remember Alan Arkin said to me – I wondered what I should do after this, should I go to Hollywood, it was filmed in Alabama – 'Well, Sondra, I always think every time I finish a job, I always think I'll never have another job.' And I remember being stunned and thinking how it's just part of the territory. So it's not that I'm so secure in it, that's not true at all. I'm probably very insecure, but I enjoy being off enough.

If you get to the black side of it, I feel that in many ways I did myself an injustice because this is such a place, this town – especially where actresses are concerned – it reminds me of when I was in school and everybody was always interested in the new girl in town, the new family moves in and everybody is always saying, 'Oooh, wow, have you seen this . . .' and they've got the daughter and the son and that's kind of the way this town is.

Once you get through that crack you have to move fast and furious because once you've been around for a while it doesn't matter your reputation or anything, they're always looking for the new girl in town. So you have to make the most of it at the time it erupts. I didn't realize that. In fact, I was so naïve, that when I auditioned for *Heart*, I thought, Gee, this was easy. I went in, I auditioned, I thought I was the best person for the part, so naturally I would get the part and then I was nominated for the Oscar and I thought, This is too easy. What is everybody talking about? I thought, That's the way it always works: you go in, you audition for the part and the person who gives the best audition gets the part. That's how dumb I was. Then after a while it began slowly to sink in that that's not the way it works at all.

Rarely it works that way. It worked in my case because they were looking for an unknown and naturally they were going to take the person they thought was the best, with no political reasons for doing anything else, but I learned quickly that was definitely not the case. After *Heart* – this is terrible – there was a picture with Noel Black directing. I thought he was such a good director. He did a film called *Pretty Poison* with Tuesday Weld and Tony Perkins and it was a marvellous little picture and he had a film at Fox called *Run, Shadow, Run* and he wanted me to do it.

At that point in my life, I was determined that in this acting game you have to act. Because the only downfall with my first film was that I realized that everybody thought I was that girl in *The Heart is a Lonely Hunter*. And I got no offers other than the exact same character and I was still high and mighty and determined to prove that I am not this character. I'm something totally different, I can be anything! And so I took this film because it gave me the opportunity to do something totally different from the first role I had done. Robert Forster was in it and in 1968 he was very hot and it seemed like a real good combination. That's when Fox released *Star*.

They lost so much money on that Julie Andrews film they didn't do a lot of advertising on the other films they had. They just pushed the picture out there and it got lost in the shuffle and a year went by with my life and career and that film did nothing. Then, I did a picture with Robert Shaw, called *Reflection of Fear*. It was a wonderful part and once again there was a lot of in-house fighting – not that I'm saying these were the greatest pictures ever made, but they were certainly good pictures worth release – but the film once again got lost out there and didn't really catch on. Every film has to have its own kind of release. So that's the way it goes; who's the next girl in town?

I didn't feel bitter about that. I felt angry at times. I still feel angry at times. I don't like to name names, but I think a lot of people get a lot of attention they don't deserve. But that's the ball game. That's just part of it. Not everything is always fair. It's a very unfair business. It's so subjective that there are no . . . nothing makes any sense.

So, I have felt angry and really annoyed at certain things and people at times. But I realize that I feel very lucky for what I have, based upon how little I put myself out. When I really sit down and talk to myself, I realize I have no complaints because I didn't go out there. If I'm going to complain at least I should exert myself. It's not that I'm lazy, it's that I don't know how to do it. It's just not a talent of mine. I remember doing a film with an actress and she was amazing. She was on the phone all day and they weren't social calls. Everything was related to business, do you know so and so, could I meet them, it was obsessive. She was perfectly happy with it. I'm not saying that's wrong. It's just that it's totally foreign to me. If I tried to do it I don't think it would work because I just don't have the talent for it. I'm not goal directed at all.

I always wanted to act, to be involved with film and I like the production end as well. I like all aspects of it. I always wanted to be involved. I don't know if I still am because I may be too far gone to change my ways but in school and always in my life I was one of those people who could learn anything. If somebody told me they were going to put me in law school, I would have been an attorney. If somebody said they were going to put me in medical school, I would have been a doctor. I'm not even saying this to compliment myself because what happens on the other side is that I don't have the goal orientation to make myself do any of those things, but I just had that knack to do anything.

I was born in Tennessee and Marion Dougherty, the casting lady, who's very well known in the business conducted a talent search for *The Heart is a Lonely Hunter* and went from city to city, primarily in the south, but also New York and Los Angeles looking for someone for the part. I heard about it, read about it in the papers and I auditioned. I drove to southern Alabama. It would make a wonderful film and Clint thought it was one of the greatest stories. I auditioned locally and then they took me to New York and I spent a few weeks there auditioning and reading with various other candidates for the other roles.

After we did the picture, I came here to Los Angeles and I've sort of been stuck here ever since. I did have a compulsion then, I wasn't alone because Gordon Anderson – my husband, we grew up together, we were like playmates when we were children – really pushed me to do it. He made me do it. I don't know if I would have done it . . . I would have done it, I think, but it seemed like one of those things that couldn't happen and it's hard to convince yourself that you could really get the part, nation-wide talent hunt and all that.

He was very interested himself, he's an artist but he was also an actor and was doing very well in New York. He actually went to New York and was studying there. I somehow felt responsible for his giving up acting because think he saw how absurd it was and he saw things that I had to go through – idiotic things most of the time – and he has so many other talents, so he just sort of fell back on those. He does miniature sculptures, mostly by commission. Many collectors sort of get on to him and they want favourite characters in a novel or film and he would sculpt these characters. Collectors are maniacs. Once they get on to you . . . He's well known among people who collect miniatures or those sorts of things. He works in porcelain. He's done a few things of me. I became Alice in Wonderland once.

Clint was totally responsible for *Sudden Impact*. It started out as a small project that he was thinking of producing and didn't even have . . . he wasn't even in it . . . it was just a small story that caught his eye and he thought it was interesting and would make a good film. He thought he'd produce it. Then the final writer who did the actual screenplay just got the idea off the wall, out of the blue of making it into a *Dirty Harry*, a murder/suspense film and suddenly it became a *Dirty Harry*. It was just a small story that probably no one would have been interested in, no one would have seen the potential. In the end, Clint did and turned it into a *Dirty Harry*.

He does that, he moves before anyone knows it. A fast draw. The films that I've been in, my two favourites are *The Outlaw Josey Wales* and *Bronco Billy*. I loved *Bronco Billy*, I thought it was very brave of Clint to make it because obviously it's not what his fans would like to see and yet people who love that kind of film, a more sophisticated audience, loved it.

But *Josey Wales* was the first film I did with Clint and I think it's a classic film. Orson Welles once said on the *Merv Griffin Show* that *The Outlaw Josey Wales* was one of the best directed films as far as he was concerned and that if Clint hadn't directed it, everyone would have called it a classic. But because Clint had a certain stigma that goes with being the kind of star that he is, he doesn't get the credit often that he deserves in the area of performing or film-making. He is simply associated with the macho superstar. But Welles said that and I was very impressed because I agreed. I think it's wonderfully directed. It's a beautiful film.

The attitude still makes me angry like it makes me angry when I don't get certain things or certain roles or certain opportunities that I think I could do a good job at. It's also part of that game that you accept certain constants in the business and I always go back to Steven Spielberg's comment when he first did *Jaws* and it was such a big hit and the picture was nominated for a Best Picture Oscar and he wasn't nominated for Best Director. I was very impressed with his comment. They were interviewing him on television and he said, 'Well, everybody loves a winner but nobody loves a winner.' And I thought, That's true.

I feel frankly that applies to Clint. He's one of the few people in the business who personally believes films are big efforts and you're only as good as the people surrounding you. Clint does, in effect, do everything in his films from start to finish. He picks the properties, produces, directs, stars and edits, picks the cast. I think people take him for granted and he's been such a big star for so many years it's just, 'Well, that's that.' That's all there is and it's not really true. For many years to come people will look at the films and say, 'Hey, that was wonderfully directed.' *Play Misty for Me* was wonderful suspense. For me one of the hardest things to accomplish – and I see films all the time – is suspense.

We met originally when I was auditioning for a role in *Breezy* which he didn't cast me in. I've always played younger. I was seventeen when I did *Heart* and played fourteen. He just wanted a maturity. We've talked about it and I say: 'How dare you not cast me in that film?' He says: 'Well, I just sensed there's a certain maturity about you that comes across in spite of yourself. There's no question you could have acted the part, but there was just a certain immaturity in this other actress that I thought was better for the film.' So that was the end of that.

Above: Former used car dealer Henry Wynberg, Maggie's second husband, whom she married in April 1985. Later he was to win a $4 million lawsuit against another lover, Elizabeth Taylor. *(REX FEATURES)*

Previous page: 'Do I feel lucky today?' Eastwood in *Magnum Force* (1973) as Dirty Harry – the Man With No Name, but clean shaven and in a neatly cut suit, shirt and conservative tie. Liberals dubbed the big .44 Magnum gun 'an angry erection'. *(WARNER BROS)*

Top: With Maggie Eastwood, née Johnson, his wife: 'Clint was only 23 and so good looking I couldn't resist him.' They married on 19 December 1953 and stayed so for 31 years. She has called herself the Woman With No Name. *(PICTORIAL PRESS)*

Above: Happy Families? With Maggie and Kyle, Eastwood's son, born in 1968, fifteen years into their marriage. Their daughter Alison was born five years later. *(REX FEATURES)*

Above: Eastwood and his longtime girlfriend, Sondra Locke, chat with Ronald Reagan's assistant, Edwin Meese, at a State Department reception before the Kennedy Center premiere of *Firefox*, 13 June 1982. *(REX FEATURES)*

Left: Sondra Locke and Eastwood in *Any Which Way You Can* (1980). His relationship with Locke helped to end his marriage at a cost to him of more than $20 million. Later she would shatter his faith in 'the loyalty of friends'. *(WARNER BROS)*

Left: Eastwood admires actresss Jo Ann Harris, who appeared with him in *The Beguiled*, at the film's screening in 1970 at the Directors' Guild Theater, Hollywood. Directed by Don Siegel, this was the first Malpaso production and audiences' first glimpse into Eastwood's personal fascination with sex and violence, of lust over innocence. *(REX FEATURES)*

Top: With his date Jacelyn Reeves, a Carmel resident, Eastwood arrives at a gathering in Los Angeles to draw attention to the Campaign for Californian Environmental Initiative of 1990. *(PICTORIAL PRESS)*

Above left: The actress Frances Fisher, another of Clint's ladies. She appeared to become a

permanent part of his life towards the end of 1990. *(PICTORIAL PRESS)*

Above: At Swifty Lazar's Oscar party with Dani Janssen, the blonde widow of Eastwood's army-days acting friend, David Janssen. There was talk that Eastwood would be husband number five. *(PICTORIAL PRESS)*

Above: Burt Reynolds and Eastwood, two of America's biggest box-office draws, appear with Sondra Locke and Loni Anderson, far right, at the world premiere of *City Heat* in Los Angeles, 5 December 1984. *(REX FEATURES)*

Right: Dani and David Janssen, star of television's *The Fugitive*, an old friend of Eastwood's from the fifties. *(REX FEATURES)*

Above: With Sondra Locke in the Eastwood classic, *The Outlaw Josey Wales*. In 1976 it was her first movie with Eastwood and one whose emotional twists echoed Eastwood's life at the time. *(BFI STILLS, POSTERS AND DESIGNS)*

Left: Sonia Braga, the Brazilian actress and sex bombshell, in *The Rookie*, where she makes love to Eastwood in a sadomasochistic scene. Braga was personally chosen by Eastwood for the role. *(BFI STILLS, POSTERS AND DESIGNS)*

Overleaf: In 1979 Eastwood and Clyde the orang-utan defied the critics and turned *Every Which Way But Loose* into the third biggest box-office success for Warner Brothers (following *The Exorcist* and the original *Superman*), earning more than $60 million – then magical numbers – at the American box office alone. *(WARNER BROS)*

At that time, I had been out here [Los Angeles] a few years and I had gotten rather blasé about a few things: an audition is an audition. I remember I wanted that part very much. It was one of the few scripts I had read since I had come to Hollywood that I really wanted and then when I heard that William Holden was playing in it, I thought, Oh, I've got to do this, I've got to do it. I was very disappointed. Joe Heims, the lady writer, wanted me to do it. She called me up and we talked and I said: 'I'm really doing my best.' It didn't work out. Clint told me later that he thought I had an interesting quality, whatever that is, and I stuck in the back of his mind and I guess the next thing that came along that he thought I might be right for was *The Outlaw Josey Wales*.

My agent got a call asking me to come in and meet him. That was it. I think basically it wasn't that large a role – it was just that it had a special quality about it – but it was the chance to work with Clint because I did admire him and what he had accomplished in the business and also I thought it might help . . . I had done all these interesting little films that hadn't gotten released and I thought this was perfect to be in a Clint Eastwood picture. Everybody will see me! It will be a commercial success! It's about time! I loved the story, the script.

And I lost my eyebrows. We were sitting around a campfire and in order to get the light we had to make the fire so enormous that when I had to stand by it during the scene, I singed my eyebrows. That was one of my best acting moments not to scream out! He's notorious for not letting actresses wear make-up. I can't get used to my face except one way. If I go to a big party I look very strange to myself with a lot of make-up, yet I'm wearing this beautiful dress, I should have on more make-up. The face doesn't go with the dress. One of my fantasies was always to do period film.

People get preconceived little niches for you and although I had a lot of work behind me when I started working with Clint several of the films weren't seen. And then you become . . . well, a lot of people think she only works with Clint and he is such a dynamic figure that it's easy for him to overwhelm, everyone wants to know what he's thinking, what he's doing, and then you become a part of that.

That did happen to me there's no denying it. I think it would be wise for me to find something uniquely my own to do. The thing about getting caught up in Clint's image is inevitable. But it hasn't happened only to me. It's happened to other performers in his pictures.

There's something I suppose that's so powerful about him and the fact that he runs his own show, that sets him apart from the rest of the business. We've talked about this. He talks about it too with the actor Andy Robinson who in the original *Dirty Harry* played the villain. Andy is a wonderful actor, but things never came round to him the way they should have but I think . . . it was a double whammy in that one because he was playing a villain and once you play the crazy villain then everybody sees you as the crazy villain.

Clint's private but it's not deliberate in any way. If it were, we didn't accomplish anything. At least not the sort of publicity I wanted. He's sort of secret as I said. Like doing the first *Dirty Harry* without anyone knowing about it until the last minute. He just doesn't like to tell anybody what he's doing. It extends to all parts of his life.

I basically am the same way. It's a bit going back to the thing of not being able to promote my own career. In a way it's the same personality quality. I don't go to cocktail parties and flow well with the traffic. I've never been very good at talking about myself which is one reason I never give interviews. I find I can talk easily with you. I don't like talking about myself. But I've always been that way. I always want to know more about the people I'm with and I start withdrawing when I'm asked questions about myself and it's not that I have big secrets, it's just the way I am.

In the beginning, when I first came to this town, I did make attempts to follow suit. I had a press agent, I had one of the best and, in my opinion, nothing worth while was accomplished. I would give these interviews, force myself and I'd read them and most of the time – and I'm not blaming the journalist because something in living 3-D is very difficult to translate into black and white, one-dimensional things – humour was lacking, inflections weren't there. Even when I would be quoted verbatim, I would say that's not me. So I just withdrew more.

Just after my first picture I came to this town and met a few people and right away I was always the vulnerable girl abused in some way or held back with a fragile character or emotionally disturbed or something like that. Then Clint used me in *The Gauntlet* in which I played a very tough girl. I like dichotomies anyway, it intrigued me. I always liked the bad seed . . .

It gives another dimension to the character to look one way and act another so I loved playing the part in *The Gauntlet*. She was tough. Well, pretty soon everybody suddenly said, 'Oh, she's tough and she's hard.' I found this really impossible. I was browsing through a bookstore one day and picked up an encyclopaedia of actors and flipped to my name to see what they're saying about me – in fact, it was an English publication – and it says: 'American actress of the type hardboiled.' I laughed and laughed. You can't win for losing!

How do I see myself? Very confused! I don't know. Sometimes I see myself as not specific enough. Because I'd always prided myself all my life on being able to be so versatile, being able to learn anything, being able to adapt to anything. I was always able to do that to the degree that I'm . . . even I don't have enough of a handle on myself. Actually I'm very down to earth, grounded, a directed person even though that sounds contradictory. But at the same time it's easy to be so many different things. I always thought that was what acting was all about and probably one of the things that attracted me to it. Then I thought, No that's not right. You have to project a certain image and be a certain way to get a certain career going. I've never done that.

Except I've got this image as sort of an extension of Clint, if you will, which is not me, so it's —

—

FOUR

Magnetic
Man

'Every woman feels she has a chance
with him.'

ACTRESS SIERRA PECHEUR IN 1980

He looks you straight in the eye when you ask about his relationship with Sondra Locke, but it is clear that after all the years his heart is not in denials. Or explanations. It happened. Girls happen.

Eastwood enjoyed the British pubs he visited with Richard Burton while filming *Where Eagles Dare* in the late sixties and when he got into partnership to open his own bar-restaurant in Carmel he gave it what he believed was a pub name, the Hog's Breath. He could have called it anything he wanted for with his association it became an instant success. There were tourists. And there were girls. Girls who looked as though they had walked out of the pages of *Vogue* or *Elle* or the Polo Lounge at the Beverley Hills Hotel. Meet a star – be a star?

The female staff there are always gracious and always loyal and usually stunning. Eastwood is a good boss. Paul Lippman was at one time a part owner with Eastwood in the Hog's Breath. He maintains Eastwood was a romantic Casanova at the pub. He chatted up all the girls. Especially the blondes. 'Clint liked small or slight women – he called them "squirts" or "shrimps" and "spinners".' According to Lippman it was lust at first sight. He said that when he and Eastwood double-dated they would talk about their girls the morning after. But he said that Eastwood said of his morning-after bedside manner: 'We don't talk – we watch cartoons.' Lippman says Eastwood liked unknown women whom he would not later accidentally meet. He maintains Eastwood had swift encounters including one with a brunette 'who taught him transcendental meditation'.

Eastwood denies the 'Dirty Clint' charge, saying: 'Other than having a couple of beers together a few times, we didn't see each other or socialize. He and his wife once owned part of the Hog's Breath but we were never close. I won't apologize for any of my behaviour because I haven't done anything wrong.' During his relationship with Locke, the actor's reputation as a ladies' man –

albeit a low-key one – never lost momentum. But in public, at Hollywood functions or at the White House, it was Locke who was on his arm.

But she was not his partner on film when he returned for the third time as Inspector Callaghan, the Mean Machine of San Francisco, in 1976. This time *Dirty Harry* got a woman partner – Tyne Daly who would later become famous world-wide as tough but tender Mary Beth Lacey in the television series *Cagney and Lacey*. In *The Enforcer* – then a topical mix of politics and terrorism following the kidnapping and subsequent bank robbery trial of heiress Patty Hearst – she got a taste of the action awaiting her on television. In the film the Mayor of San Francisco is kidnapped and Harry and Daly's Detective Kate Moore are on alert. Daly's Moore dies – another partner gone for Dirty Harry. Victim or not, it was a good scene-stealing role and she recalls:

> *I was really proud of my work on* The Enforcer *because I have to act even more than usual. I just can't stand the sight of guns but I didn't want to turn down the chance to play opposite Clint. I just had to swallow my feelings, look into his eyes and get on with the show. Clint taught me to handle guns like an expert. Everything I did on* Cagney and Lacey *I learned from him. He's a good teacher.*

And frugal. He's not known as 'skinClint' for nothing. During *The Enforcer* a blue Cutlass car had ploughed through a store window. In 1977 the same car – engine removed – is finally to go out of service. Eastwood was star and director of *The Gauntlet* and on location in the Nevada desert near Las Vegas here was one more special effect. On cue the car blows, the roof spinning through the smoke with other debris as flames played around the dummy-victim in the driving seat. Eastwood is still to survive a police ambush, a car bombing, a Stateline shoot-out, a helicopter attack, a showdown with a motorcycle gang, a flight on a freight train – and that's before he hijacks a Greyhound bus and drives through town with 300 policemen blasting at him with machine guns. Just another Clint Eastwood love story.

He plays Arizona cop Ben Shockey in *The Gauntlet* who is nowhere near as smart as Dirty Harry and likes the bottle too much. He is trying to get prostitute Gus Mally, played by Sondra Locke, back from Vegas to Phoenix to be the key witness in a mob trial. Speaking on location then she said: 'You can't say there are no good roles for women when you see this. She's very feisty – she's got a different nature from mine.' So, of course, has Eastwood. These were the early days of their romance. She talked about him sometimes in strange contradictions. 'He's one of the most sensitive, gentlest men in the world – with the most horrifying temper.' She told the story of how he had punched a recalcitrant horse in the jaw during the filming of *Josey Wales* and then went on:

Yet he wouldn't kill spiders – he helped me get over my fear of them. I have the greatest amount of respect, admiration and fondness for him and I think it's mutual. I love working with him but there's nothing specific in the works . . . Nobody is going to complain about playing opposite Clint as a romantic lover on screen.

Eastwood was quizzed about her then and smiled a reply: 'Good spontaneity.' He also defended his women in films: 'When feminism came in I was one of the early targets. What they didn't notice was how many of my films have good roles for strong women. Sondra in *The Gauntlet* had more to say than I did. And despite the fact that the character is a hooker we didn't cast for some busty, gum-chewing, dumb blonde. We made her an intelligent, strong woman. I'd never cast myself opposite a woman who was there merely for sex appeal. I cast it a little off. Good casting would be to make her a princess – she *is* a princess. But to cast as a hooker – that's the twist.'

It was not an argument feminists readily accepted. Eastwood's attitude to that was much the same as to the gossip about him and his leading lady. Also, there was the question of Maggie Eastwood and Locke's husband, Gordon Anderson. Locke maintained in 1977: 'Gordon and I don't sit down and talk about it. He figures if there's any truth to it, I'll be the first to tell him. If there's anything to know, he'll know it.'

Nevertheless, it was Eastwood she visited in Carmel. Or went skiing with in Vail, Colorado or the Sun Valley Resort near Ketchum, Idaho. We might suggest the situation suited Eastwood. It took pressure off him to get divorced. It gave him time to play pub playboy at the Hog's Breath. Man, wife, mistress – recall Sir James Goldsmith's famous warning: 'When a man marries a mistress, it creates a vacancy.'

Others said the situation was fine by Sondra Locke because it took the pressure off her – she was frightened of embarrassing her strict Baptist parents in Wartrace, Tennessee. Even after all the publicity, Sondra Locke's mother, Pauline, said at her home:

Sondra tells me these rumours about her and Clint are not true and for us not to pay any attention to them. Sondra and Gordon are still in love and are still married and living together – no matter what people say about her and Clint. And there's no talk of divorce.

A curious set-up. Especially when we were later to learn that during her relationship with Eastwood the actress would at times sleep over with her husband. It was reported in America and never denied that the trio would go out on dates together along with lots of other Odd Couple gossip.

In 1978 Eastwood/Locke were an established movie team when they made *Every Which Way But Loose*. It was a change of pace for the actor. He played a laid-back truck driver, Philo Beddoe, who is chasing Locke's country-and-western singer, Lynne Halsey-Taylor, across America. To finance the trip he has the help of friends Clyde, an orang-utan, and Orville played by Eastwood repertory-company member Geoffrey Lewis. They start bar-room brawls – Eastwood's the fighter – and bet their travel money on the results.

Eastwood admits Clyde was not always easy to work with. A little temperamental? 'Orang-utans are shy and standoffish – they're not like chimpanzees who are total extroverts. With Clyde what we'd do was simple: I'd give him half a can of beer, he'd relax, and we'd do the scene. We had to get it right on the first scene though because Clyde didn't have much patience.'

What about Eastwood's kissing scenes with Clyde? Full on the lips stuff? 'You've got to understand that people get sort of attached to Clyde. Besides, Clyde is a very warm-lipped primate. They say you should never play a scene with a child actor or an animal – they'll steal the scene every time. But at that stage in my career I thought, What the hell – I'll take a chance with an orang-utan.'

. . .

In 1979, Clint Eastwood had a new love in his life – a $100,000 red Ferrari, a competition car that you push to the limit. A speed machine. He took a high performance driving course at an exclusive California school. He was still involved with Sondra Locke. He and Maggie Eastwood separated in January 1979, after twenty-six years of marriage.

Then Eastwood and Clyde, the orang-utan, defied the critics and turned *Every Which Way But Loose* into the third biggest box-office success for Warner Brothers (following *The Exorcist* and the original *Superman*) earning more than $60 million – then magical numbers – at the American box office alone. The film went on to be equally successful in Europe and in 1992 was still a money-maker on video and television. He also planned to team up again with Don Siegel, who would direct Eastwood in *Escape from Alcatraz* – a fact-based tale of convicts doing what was regarded as the impossible: getting free from the prison known as The Rock that sits out so bleakly and ominously in San Francisco Bay.

Eastwood turned forty-nine years of age in 1979. It was all classic male menopause. Younger girl. Separation from wife. Proving that age is no limit to achievement, even the films were good ol' boy action-packed manhood movies. It was like Jack Palance at the 1992 Oscars doing one-arm push-ups before a television audience of one billion viewers to show that, even at seventy-two, he didn't need a health certificate to work. But Hollywood is very much that way – they think insurance, they concern themselves about the bottom line, the profit and the loss of such should a star die or be unable to complete a film. For an action star like Eastwood the age of forty-nine must have indeed been dangerous. So he did dangerous things. In Hollywood they often call him the 'meno-Porsche'.

By the spring of 1979 Eastwood had raced with another star driver, Paul Newman, at Riverside Raceway in California and had arranged to take a course at Bob Bondurant's School of High Performance Driving in Northern California. It is a place often used to train drivers of international businessmen and politicians to avoid kidnap in high-speed chases. It also gives exclusive courses to laymen. Eastwood took a five-day course along with acting friends Gene Hackman and James Brolin.

At the Bondurant School they said Eastwood was very dedicated. 'He was a good, clever driver – careful but not afraid to take risks,' said an instructor who had to be persuaded to admit that Eastwood even attended the school. 'We don't really like to comment on clients for security reasons, but it's sometime ago. It's a real hazardous course.'

And so, of course, is marriage. Maggie Eastwood made the decision to separate after all the loyal years. She didn't ask for a divorce then. Maybe it was just a way to tell her husband that she had needs too. Eastwood was totally taken aback by her request for a separation. He thought things were fine. 'Like everyone else, we had our good times and our bad times,' she reflected later.

Eastwood moved out of their marital home, a giant spread of a place near Carmel with priceless views over the Pacific and a real-estate price then of $5 million and now in 1992 – despite recession – probably worth twice that sum. He rented a house in Hollywood to get on with making *Escape from Alcatraz*, both on the sound stages and on location at the prison which no longer functions as a jail but as a tourist attraction.

Eastwood himself was by now a major attraction on the big and small screen. After he and Maggie Eastwood separated he was asked in a major American television interview with Barbara Walters about it. There was much preamble about what was or wasn't the case. Eastwood replied: 'I'm legally separated if that's what you mean. People have problems within marriages. Everybody has them and some people manage to resolve them or work them out and others don't. Whether she helped me or I helped her – I mean, we have a very good relationship. She and I are probably better friends and having much more amiable conversations, more sensible conversations about philosophical differences or agreements now than we ever have.'

Walters asked: 'Is Sondra Locke the number one relationship in your life?'

Eastwood replied: 'She's a very extraordinary girl, a very intelligent girl, very smart. I enjoy her very much as an actress and personally and I . . . she's one of my number one friends. She's just a very special person.'

Although he's not yet divorced, he's asked: 'Can you imagine remarrying?'

'I'm not a person who preplans life. I preplan as far as films and the education of the kids and what not, but I think one has to be relaxed about life.'

Walters asked him about sex appeal, about why women throw themselves at him and went on: 'Yet, you don't think you're sexy?'

'Do you fool around on the first date?' asked Eastwood.

A flustered and reddening Walters tried to bluff: 'I could do this interview all day,' she replies, stumbling. Eastwood offered his enigmatic smile.

But on location at The Rock he was grim in the inhuman world which had been created again for Don Siegel's cameras. Everything about the movie was tough and it was clear Eastwood was out to prove himself. In the film he plays Frank Morris who, on 18 January 1960, arrived at Alcatraz, California's island prison. Morris had escaped from several prisons. In the first scenes we see the Warden – Patrick McGoohan – telling him he won't escape from Alcatraz. When a pair of brothers Morris knows arrive at the maximum-security prison, they begin to plan just that. The scheme is elaborate. Using makeshift tools, they manage to get through the ventilation grilles leading from their cells to a shaft which goes to the roof. They make dummy heads for their bunks – heads with human hair from the prison barber shop. Raincoats strengthened with contact cement work as a base for their gateway shaft. On 11 June 1962, they went for it. Frank Morris and Clarence and John Anglin were never heard of again. Authorities believed they would find their bodies in the icy waters of San Francisco Bay. They didn't. Their escape – or death? – remains the only unsolved case in the prison's history. Within a year the prison had been closed.

The story fascinated Richard Tuggle. Al Capone had been imprisoned there and Richard Stroud – The Birdman of Alcatraz – was another infamous inmate. But when Tuggle heard the tale of the escape Frank Morris masterminded, he asked: Has anyone made a movie about this? His question was to team him with Eastwood – a chance but pivotal combination.

Tuggle only decided to write a screenplay of the story after he lost his job as an editor at a San Francisco health magazine. He then approached publishers McGraw-Hill who had the rights to a story based on the incident. Amazingly, the novice Tuggle managed to persuade them to give up all film rights to the story. The first-time film writer heard that Don Siegel had once been interested in the project and the chain to Eastwood – the actor whose twenty-eight films to that time had earned more than half a billion dollars – began. Within five years Tuggle would be directing his own screenplay *Tightrope* which showed Eastwood delving into the dark side of one man's sexuality playing a very different dirty detective.

But in 1980 there were memories of the past. American television viewers voted *Rawhide* the golden-oldie series they would most like to see again. By then Eastwood, at fifty, was playing a different kind of cowboy called Bronco Billy. He never thought he would make a film like *Escape from Alcatraz* explaining: 'I surprised myself. I never was too big on prison movies even as a kid, too much confinement, not enough sprawl to them. But there was a real suspense story in *Alcatraz* – a guy with no education but smart enough to scheme himself off the Rock. I liked it.'

'The same way I liked *Bronco Billy* right away – it's the sort of film Frank Capra might have made about a romantic, dreamy bunch of losers getting their act together. So, I look at the whole picture, not just my role in it. I look for an entertaining story. When I go to the movies, I go for the action, the laughs, then I have a few beers. I don't go to intellectualize. If you analyse too much of anything in this life, you'll analyse your way right out of it.'

Eastwood made *Bronco Billy* on location in Boise, Idaho. Bronco Billy is a poor man's Buffalo Bill with a rather dog-eared Western show. As the title character, Eastwood sported pearl-handled six-shooters and a white rodeo shirt. Sondra Locke played runaway heiress Antoinette Lily who joins this particular circus.

Her relatives are trying to cheat her out of her inheritance. Bronco Billy's trying to show her the ropes. Although it did not have major box-office impact – comparable to an Eastwood shoot 'em up – it was a memorable, breakaway film for him. And for it he again rounded up some of the usual suspects including Geoffrey Lewis. Lewis, the father of Juliette Lewis who was nominated as 1992 Best Supporting Actress for her role in director Martin Scorsese's remake of *Cape Fear*, played a scheming fortune hunter in *Bronco Billy*.

Lewis also appeared in *High Plains Drifter, Every Which Way But Loose* and *Any Which Way You Can* – in the latter two movies as Eastwood's good ol' boy buddy Orville. 'Working with Clint is always a pleasure,' says the actor who lives in California's San Fernando Valley. 'There is no giant star ego thing about him – you just go in there and sweep up the work and then relax. He doesn't make a song and dance out of it.'

'Clint's kind of a guru director,' says Sam Bottoms who is another Eastwood company regular. Bottoms – brother Timothy and Joseph are also actors – goes on:

He gets this laid-back Zen feeling to come over the set. And, of course, as an actor, he can do just about any role he picks for himself. I'll make a prediction though – I don't think Clint will ever hang up his guns. He'll go out blazing.

'Clint likes to shoot films fast and clean,' says Bob Daley who has been Eastwood's longtime producer. 'He expects a lot from himself and he expects others to measure up and keep pace with him.' Back when they were making *Bronco Billy* – the character is really a New Jersey show salesman who promotes himself as The Fastest Gun in the West – they all realized they were witnessing a new phase in Eastwood's life, reflected in the new style and attitude of the film. One of its songs – a duet by country-and-western star Merle Haggard and Eastwood titled 'Bar Room Buddies' – made America's Top Forty country-and-western best selling charts in

1980. At fifty, he seemed to have moved on – escaped the chains of middle age. He was asked a question then and replied: 'Happy? I *am* happy. Many people with everything are too complicated to be happy. I'm not.' Oh, really?

.   .   .

As part of his Western show, Bronco Billy would shoot blindfolded at a busty blonde being spun furiously around on a Wheel of Fortune. The kinky implications of the skimpily clothed girl strapped down on the wheel were clear to Eastwood the man – and the director. 'Oh, sure,' he said on the film set when a film technician teased him about it and then he added smiling: 'We've been hustlin' gals for this wheel all week.'

Tesse Richards who has a Monroe bosom and breathy voice was 'the gal on the wheel'. It didn't take a lot of persuading to get her up there. Just listen to her. Breathlessly:

Clint has a certain star quality. He's got that mystery in his eyes, a distant twinkle. And he wasn't at all like the tough guy I imagined. There's a gentleness about him that makes him very sexy. He's got a rugged boy look, but he's very sensitive. He can look fierce one moment and loving the next. He's very soft-spoken but at the same time he's so overwhelming that you can actually be afraid of him. Yet you immediately feel you can trust him. He makes you feel part of the family.

Sierra Pecheur played an Indian squaw in *Bronco Billy*:

When I first encountered Clint the big surprise was his humour. I had no idea how rascally he is. He has this little air of devilry right between his eyes. He's very playful, a real charmer. Macho doesn't really apply to Clint. He's strong, yes, but not macho. There's a finesse to him. I don't mean effete – I mean, there's a nice delicate feeling of sensitivity to him even when he's being ferocious. And he's definitely sexy – though maybe magnetic is a better word. Not a cold kind of magnetism but a playful, pleasure-

filled delicious kind of energy of life. To women, he's got romantic presence, an essence.

There's an old saying about Clint Eastwood – every woman feels she has a chance with him. It's not blatant sexuality. It's more in the possibilities than in anything overt.

They like him, they really like him. Also, there's an old story about Eastwood being approached by a man who offers him his girlfriend for the night saying: 'Only for you, Clint. You're the only other guy in the world I'd want her to make it with.' Eastwood makes an excuse and leaves the conversation.

Jack Green was the camera operator on a string of Eastwood films going back to *The Gauntlet* and including *Bronco Billy* and more recently *White Hunter, Black Heart* and *The Rookie* in 1990. Green was promoted to Director of Photography for Eastwood's return to the period Western with *Unforgiven,* which was filmed in Canada and went into cinemas in America and Europe late in 1992. An amiable man, he talked on location in Savannah, Georgia while he was Director of Photography for Lizzie Borden's film *Love Crimes.* Eastwood was not involved in that movie but would have liked the atmosphere, the one moment coy and then sexually aggressive Southern ladies. Says Green:

Clint likes to have close people close to him. There's a certain security in that. I think there's about fifteen of us who have worked on most of the movies. He's not a show-off or anything like that. If he's having beers with the guys that's exactly what he's doing. He's not out to impress people. Of course, he doesn't have to. The ladies? He doesn't have to impress them either.

But Eastwood the Casanova was having problems with Sondra Locke in late 1980. He had taken off skiing in Vail, Colorado, where he reportedly openly dated several girls at the resort – 'hip pocket rockets'. One local businessman recalls,

At the busiest bar in town, Shadows, he invited women to sit at his table while other girls were hanging over the back of his chair.

He loved all the attention he was getting. Girls were slipping him phone numbers and he was smiling and laughing and loving it all. No matter where he went in town, he had a beautiful woman on each arm.

This apparently led to a short separation between the couple. Later, it would be revealed there was more involved than Eastwood playing the pub playboy.

At the same time, Maggie Eastwood was trying to get on with her life and the man she chose to share it was former used-car dealer Henry Wynberg. Wynberg, who turned fifty-eight in 1992, was the man who squired Elizabeth Taylor between her two marriages to the late Richard Burton. Famous names. Taylor. Eastwood. Wynberg? The man whose association with Taylor had made him the most famous second-hand car salesman of all time became 'an international millionaire', a 'millionaire playboy', and was dubbed a string of other meaningless phrases. At the time he was immodestly dignified about it: 'I'm just a nice-looking ex-used-car salesman who happened to meet a charming lady.'

When he was fined $1000 after pleading no contest to charges that he turned back odometers on four cars he sold between July 1972 and May 1973, Wynberg then was describing himself as active in 'various stages of entertainment'. After his relationship with Taylor ended in 1975 he was accused of having sex with four girls aged fifteen to seventeen on several occasions at his then Beverley Hills home. He was also charged with providing the under-age-of-consent girls with drugs and alcohol. Then an aspiring photographer – years later, in 1990, he sold private pictures of Elizabeth Taylor to European magazines – there was another charge of taking pictures of 'a sexual nature' of the girls. Wynberg pleaded guilty in 1977 to statutory rape of a sixteen-year-old girl and admitted giving drugs to four high-school girls in return for sex. He was convicted on all counts and sentenced to ninety days in jail.

In October 1980, he was saying in California that he had been with Maggie Eastwood for eighteen months: 'I'm happy with Maggie but we've been trying to keep it secret. We first met at a dinner party in Beverley Hills. It was at the home of a mutual friend and we've been together ever since.' Wynberg would seem a strange choice to step into Clint Eastwood's shoes. But, he was attentive. They played tennis together. They skied together. They went swimming together.

Ironically, he met Maggie Eastwood at a dinner party after the collapse of her marriage. He met Taylor at the home of President John Kennedy's one-time brother-in-law, the late British actor and alcoholic Peter Lawford, after her first failed matrimonial merriment with Burton. It may not have been merry widows but the Dutch-born Wynberg who moved to America when he was seventeen years old seemed to have a grasp of being in the right seat at the right table at the right time. He was sitting next to Maggie Eastwood for quite some time. He said then:

Elizabeth Taylor is a very moral and loyal lady and I have found Maggie to be the same.

I find Maggie extremely mellow and relaxed in her attitude to life – she is a nice, stable influence on me. I think we all need a stable influence if we can find one. There are too many people partying around and I have been through all that nonsense. There is nothing quite as nice as a quiet little dinner at home . . . and going to bed early is wonderful.

When Wynberg was saying these things in 1980, there was much speculation of a Clint and Maggie Eastwood divorce. The arithmetic of such a divorce argued that Maggie Eastwood would receive something more than $25 million for an end to her long marriage to the world's richest star. The divorce wasn't about to happen – yet.

Clint Eastwood was bemused by all of it. But, even if it was begrudgingly, he had to admit that his wife seemed happy and there were no objections to his children travelling abroad on holiday with their mother and Wynberg. Except that he was about to ground his son Kyle as he wanted him to co-star in a new movie with him. He had completed *Any Which Way You Can* as well as *Bronco Billy* in 1980. Even for hard-working Eastwood there had to be a time to breathe before starting *Honkytonk Man* in 1982.

In *Honkytonk Man* Eastwood played Red Stovall a hard-drinking Depression Days country-and-western singer trying to get success before the late surges of tuberculosis finish his chances. Sounds corny? It certainly would not be the sort of material you would gamely walk into a Hollywood conference with, offering a grin and: 'Hey, have I got something for Clint.' But, remember, this is a changed man. Eastwood was directing. Sondra Locke, who does not appear in the film, was coach for Kyle Eastwood when he was cast as his father's nephew in the film. It's another familiar story – the youngster trying to keep the elder on the straight and narrow path. Eastwood recalled of his son: 'He listened well and thought out the part. When he didn't, I was there to remind him.'

Nepotism, you ask? Dangerous? Rejection? Ego problems later in life? Clint Eastwood sees none of that: 'He's a very natural kid and he's been totally immersed in film. He was always obsessed with it. When other kids would be watching cartoons, he'd be watching *Of Mice and Men* – the original 1939 version. That's why I thought he'd be able to handle that size of a part. Kyle kept asking me to let him have a part in a film and I realized that the boy in *Honkytonk Man* was just his age at the time so I let him have a go.'

Kyle Eastwood was fourteen years old when he co-starred (literally in the billing) with his father and he recalls the early teenager reaction: 'I liked stealing the chickens. I liked driving the car.'

Legendary country-and-western singer Marty Robbins recorded the title song but suffered a fatal heart attack before the film was released in cinemas. But the music was part of the new Eastwood following his 'Bar Room Buddies' duet with Merle Haggard and Eddie Rabbitt's *Every Which Way But Loose*. Eastwood was happy with the film. The critics were not. And, more hurtful, neither were audiences. The film went into cinemas a few months after *Firefox* which was also made in 1982. In *Firefox* director Eastwood starred himself as a superhero American-agent pilot who goes into Russia to steal a supersonic, super-duper Soviet plane. (Eastwood had last played a pilot in 1955's *Tarantula*, when he was called upon heroically to bomb the giant spider.) The film had spectacular special effects but not much affect with audiences. Eastwood was not ruffled by two misses in a row.

'It's a little ironic,' he said then, 'that some of the critics who didn't like what I was doing in the sixties say they don't like what I'm doing now because it's not as good as the stuff I was doing in the sixties. They said Harry was on the edge of being a fascist. Now they ask why I'm not going to do Dirty Harry again. But where would you take him now? Without the very good combination and the very good writing the *Harry* films had, there's no point in doing it again now except for monetary reasons.' And Clint Eastwood is a most practical man. Dirty Harry returned in 1983 in the film *Sudden Impact*. Eastwood had found another reason than money to make it – a feminist reason. The killer is a woman. And played by, guess who?

Forget good ol' boy Clint. On a random count Dirty Harry blows away fourteen problem people – aka 'scum' – during the film and falls in love with Sondra Locke who kills three men and a woman in revenge for a gang rape a decade earlier. There is no country-and-western soundtrack with this film in which Top Forty Hits have an altogether different meaning. This is Dirty Harry gone astray. Inspector Harry seems to be flaying out at everything. It was 1983 and it seems Eastwood was lashing at his own devils. Sondra Locke is an anguished painter, after the man who raped her and her sister. When she finds them, she shoots them in the groin. And then in the head. Boom, boom! Is this an eye for an eye and an ear for an ear? What it was was a vigilante film – the fourth and most exploitative of the *Harry* series. Eastwood and Locke are teamed as soul mates, Dirty Harry and Dirty Harriet, in the most violent lurid film. It was also an instant hit, the most successful of the *Dirty Harry* films and earned more than $100 million within weeks.

Critical redemption for Eastwood was only a short time away. In *Tightrope* in 1984 he played Detective Wes Block of New Orleans who wanders the sexual, nocturnal playground of that city. 'Go on, make my night,' Detective Wes might have said to the many ladies of the evening he encounters. Eastwood protégé Richard Tuggle's film is set in the city's French quarter where someone is murdering prostitutes – prostitutes with a liking for sado-masochistic sex. In the tradition of film noir, the thrust of the tale is that the criminal is a distorted image of the cop. When Eastwood's Wes Block visits the brothels and finds the hookers he meets seductive he holds back, agonizes and then gives in to his compulsions. But the girls he has sex with start getting murdered and he must confront his own demons, his double nature, his dark side.

Block is shown as a single parent – 'My wife didn't want tenderness' – bringing up two blonde daughters one of whom is played by nine-year-old Alison Eastwood. ('I thought it was only fair to let her have a turn at being in a film, too.') He's a man trying his best to do the decent thing. Then he has to investigate the killings at night . . . and it's a tour of erotic specialities with the girls dangling delights like handcuffs. And producing whips and vibrators and lots of symbolism with a red lollipop.

The critics loved the bondage and kinks, Eastwood/Block rubbing himself all over with baby oil and handcuffing a young lady to a bedpost . . . finally, with Dirty Wes, he was a true *auteur*.

Genevieve Bujold plays Beryl who runs a help centre for rape victims. She understands Block – and the killer. When she and Block become lovers, she even offers to put the handcuffs on for him but he unlocks them. Wes Block no longer wants total control.

Eastwood was in control, at least professionally. In 1984 he was named the world's top box-office star for the second year in a row. He had knocked his old friend Burt Reynolds off the top spot in 1983 making cinema history – it was his sixteenth appearance on the Top Ten list which was more than any living star. There were no hard feelings from Reynolds. He and Eastwood were going to make a film together in a dazzling display of superstar power. But that top spot made a difference financially. Eastwood was paid $5 million and Reynolds $4 million to make *City Heat*. The film was to change both their lives. Reynolds would lose his star power and find his whole life irrevocably changed. And Eastwood would officially lose his wife – he and Maggie Eastwood finally agreed to divorce in 1984 after thirty-one years of marriage.

FIVE

Riding High

'There are two American art forms, the Western and jazz. It's funny how Americans don't support either of them any more.'

CLINT EASTWOOD ON AMERICA

Eastwood felt *Tightrope* had been tough going and decided his next film should be fun. *City Heat* sounded just that and for the first time in his career he agreed to be packaged with another star. You can see the potential of Eastwood and Reynolds, the two biggest box-office stars in the world – a modern-day Clark Gable and Spencer Tracy or James Cagney and Pat O'Brien partnership, the charisma of a friendly enemy relationship.

The plot had them caught between rival mobs during the thirties – a comic romp with bullets flying all over the place with the laughs. It was to be directed by Blake *Pink Panther* Edwards who also wrote the script but before a camera was even loaded he walked away from the project and actor/director Richard *Mermaids* Benjamin took over. Eastwood says he had asked Edwards to make some character changes but nothing was done: 'I think it ended amicably. At least, it did on my part. I said: "I'll step back." The studio said: "No, no, we don't want you and Burt to step back."'

Later, they probably wished they had. This potential fire-cracker of a movie went off like a damp squib. It was more than just a box-office disaster for Reynolds. During the filming of *City Heat* he was accidentally hit on the face. He thought he had broken his jaw. It was much worse. The bash he received during the fight scene developed into temporomandibular joint disorder (TMJ), affecting his balance and sensory perceptions. He lived on soup and got thinner and thinner. Reynolds says:

> *People are willing to believe I had AIDS because it was just too good a rumour to let go. I'm sure it started with two gay hairdressers as a joke: 'Charlie Bronson, Clint Eastwood and Burt Reynolds have AIDS . . .' and when I wasn't showing up and got thin.*

The AIDS rumour began years of frustration and anger but he finally found success again in 1992 with *Evening Shade*.

While Burt Reynolds had been struggling to restart his career, his longtime friend's wife Maggie Eastwood was considering marriage to Henry Wynberg who had stuck to her like a limpet since they first met. But she still wasn't a 'free' woman. In the summer of 1984, she filed for divorce. The settlement – she and Eastwood had agreed to a property settlement four years earlier – was not to be discussed but sources say that given the property market of the early eighties, the divorce package provided Maggie Eastwood with around $28 million.

'She realized that she and Clint weren't getting any younger and she wanted them both to be free to remarry,' a friend in Carmel said. There was another less generous theory from a man who has known both Eastwood and his former wife for many years:

> She lost hope that Clint would get tired of Sondra and go back to her. She realized they would no longer live as husband and wife again so why stay married? But she likes having a man around the house and that's why she married Wynberg.

Eastwood, of course, didn't marry Sondra Locke. Instead, in September 1984, he was on location in Sun Valley, Idaho starring in and directing *Pale Rider*, his first pure Western since *The Outlaw Josey Wales* in 1976. The film takes place during the California gold rush of 1850. Eastwood is the anonymous stranger wearing a preacher's outfit and a couple of weeks' worth of beard. He goes to the aid of a bunch of independent miners who are being muscled out of their claims by a conglomerate mining concern. Some saw the film as the other side of *High Plains Drifter* in which Eastwood's character represented the devil, whereas this time the allegory cast him as one of God's avengers. Simpler folk thought it simply a homage to director George Stevens' 1953 landmark Western *Shane* which starred Alan Ladd, Jean Arthur, Van Heflin and Jack Palance.

The stars in *Pale Rider* included Sean Penn's brother, Chris, as one of the bad guys. 'It was,' he recalled, 'a dream come true. I'd seen 'very Clint Eastwood film there is and had wanted to do a Western since I was a kid. I even got to tell Clint to get out of town.' Also in the cast were Michael Moriarty and Carrie Snodgress – on the side of good – and giant Richard Kiel who was memorable as James Bond villain Jaws.

Eastwood made quite an impression on Sun Valley (pop: 12,000) especially during the slack business period between the end of summer and the beginning of the ski season. And time on location gave an insight to Eastwood at work and the demands and pressures he puts on his team. On *Pale Rider*, the cast and crew numbered more than 100 people: he took his own village with him.

It was about the end of August 1984, recalled Kathy Wygle, director of the Laughing Stock Theatre Company, that she was first contacted by a casting director from Warner Brothers Studios in Los Angeles: 'They asked if I would like to assist them in casting some minor roles in a Clint Eastwood movie that would be shooting up here,' she recalled. 'I had about five days to get four people for [each of] fourteen roles.' Wygle strolled around town until she found people with the right look: 'We were able to cast three speaking roles and lots of featured extras.'

Loren Adkins, a Wygle discovery, called the mining set 'real authentic'. The eighty-year-old retired Forest Service employee had reason to know – he'd been there. 'I was six years old in 1916 and my dad ran a butcher shop in Placerville [California]. I remember the screens they used to wash gold-laden dirt down the hills.' Up on the hillside, smoke puffed out from tin chimneys on a cluster of weathered wood shacks. At that point in the filming schedule, the mining camp had been completely pillaged by the bad guys. Smoke still rose from abandoned campfires.

Paul Calabria, who with partner Karen Dew handled the set's smaller livestock, was 'chicken wrangling', alternately unleashing a dozen chickens from their pen when a scene was shot, then gathering them up again when it stopped. 'These aren't trained to come when they're called, like the chickens we keep in Los Angeles,' Calabria explained good-humouredly. 'These are "non-pros"' (Hollywood talk for 'not in the business'). He threw his feathered charges a baleful look, adding, 'When we first let this batch go, they went *everywhere* – we were picking them out of trees!' Then he grinned. 'Now they're much better, though. They're becoming Hollywood chickens . . . they want more money.'

Eastwood, in full costume – boots, spurs, black vest, gray shirt – moved quietly about, setting up the last shots of what had been a long week of ten-hour days. Accompanying him was his son Kyle, visiting for the weekend. Eastwood moved from actor to actor, giving directions for the next scene. On set, as the cameras rolled, Eastwood and Michael Moriarty began methodically to smash a huge boulder with heavy sledgehammers, soon to be joined by other miners. After about 10 strokes, the director stopped and, wiping his brow, said calmly, 'Well, that's enough of that.'

The atmosphere surrounding the actual filming may have been calm and steady, but several miles away, on the set where the cast and crew would move in a week, the pace was breakneck. The construction crew had been at work for a month, building a small Western town from scratch. This was not to be just a one-dimensional, false-façade town either; the buildings would be used inside and out. One crew member paused just long enough to explain, 'Hey, we gotta move fast – Clint's right on our butts.'

The twelve buildings stood in various stages of readiness. Some were finished outside but needed furnishing; others were still in the bare-frame stage. Workers scrambled around to the cacophony of hammering, drilling and sawing that obliterated anything but the loudest of conversations. Three commercial truck/trailer rigs stood nearby, overflowing with set dressings, and lumber was strewn everywhere. Production designer Edward

Carfagno, moving quickly in and out of the various locations, was an elusive target. He finally was located in the set's dry goods store inspecting the picks, sledgehammers, mining pans and everything else that an 1850 mining town would carry. He appeared unruffled by the impending deadline. 'We'll get it done in time,' he said calmly, 'but we actually needed more like five or six weeks.'

Although a sign posted 100 yards down the road advised sightseers to keep out, no less than three different groups of locals circled the site in an hour. One contingent, a tiny troop of cub scouts, hiked up behind one of the buildings, accompanied by den mothers Teri Boderstab and Pat Peebles. 'One of their classmates is in the movie, so we thought it would be fun to bring them up here for their first meeting of the year,' Peebles explained. 'This movie is the talk of the town!' Cub business at that moment concerned the signs proclaiming the town LeHood, California. 'Now why do you think Mr Eastwood came to Idaho to make a movie about California?' Boderstab asked her charges, who had no trouble with the answer.

'Idaho looks more Western!'

'It's more natural.'

'Because there's too much smog in California!'

In the meantime the cubs speculated among themselves about Clint. 'It's been "Clint" this and "Clint" that all the way up here,' Peebles said, laughing. 'You'd think they were personal friends of his.' Their speculation concerned Eastwood's mode of transportation, whether his limousine would be able to make the eight-mile trip up the rutted dirt road.

'No, Clint'll fly in by helicopter,' said one scout. After all, they reasoned, he was a star. The star chuckled when told of the scout's various speculations during a lunch break the next day. 'I'm the guy who asks not to use limos!'

Eastwood seemed to have no problem doing a Western nine years out of the saddle. 'Isn't it beautiful here! Ninety per cent of my last pictures have been shot at night. Here we'll only have two night shots.'

Why a Western? Why now?

'Two fellows I'd used before came to me several years ago with this idea, and I liked it and gave them some ideas. I didn't know exactly when we'd shoot, but I do like fall – the sun's low and the light's good.'

Eastwood was matter-of-fact about his much discussed rapid directorial style, which Richard Kiel figured came from his work with Sergio Leone. 'Actually, Leone is slower than I am. I give a lot of the credit to Don Siegel [who directed Eastwood in *Two Mules for Sister Sara*, *The Beguiled*, *Dirty Harry* and *Escape from Alcatraz*]. He was always organized for speed.' He pondered it for a second, then added, 'But you learn from everyone you work with. I'm surrounded by the best crew around, and we all like to move at the same tempo. I think if the director is slow and ponderous, it can hurt the final product. The movie might not be as satisfying and, besides,' he shrugged, 'I'd get bored.'

In Hollywood, Eastwood's longtime producer Fritz Manes – taking time away from the location to help with the trailer for *City Heat*, the videocassette of *Tightrope* and the television version of *Sudden Impact* – offered his thoughts on *Pale Rider* and Westerns. 'We've been sitting on *Pale Rider* since '78 or '79. There were other things we thought required more urgency as far as filming went, since they were fairly timely, such as *Firefox*.'

Manes said Eastwood had always been fairly

obsessed with the project. His whole bent was Westerns from the start, and I can't tell you how many fans have asked him or written to ask when he would do a Western again. You can't feel as secure with Pale Rider *as you would with, say, a sequel to* Dirty Harry. *However, my feeling is that there's going to be no problem.*

He shrugged.

*I guess themes just run in cycles . . . detective movies, then cars,
drugs, outer space and whatever. But everybody loves cowboys.
They know the hero always comes out on top – it gives people a
good fantasy to live with.*

Eleven years before *Pale Rider* was made Eastwood galloped
across the world's cinema screens in a film that many regard not just
as a fantasy but as the ultimate one and *the* last great Western ever
made. *The Outlaw Josey Wales* was more than the white-hat-black-
hat-tall-in-the-saddle-good-versus-evil Western. Arguably, no one
but Eastwood could have pulled off *Pale Rider* in the middle of the
1980s or maybe even in the past couple of decades. *Shane* had been
more than thirty years ago and the 1985 update would seem all too
elliptical for the MTV generation. In 1976, Eastwood also went up
against the odds with *Josey Wales* – Westerns in the seventies were
financial leprosy as far as Hollywood was concerned and equally
contagious – but he gambled on his edge: his instinct. And he won.

In 1992 as his fans anticipated the release of *Unforgiven*, a
new video-marketing gimmick in America was introduced. The
tapes went on sale at supermarket check-out counters and the price
on average is around $9.99. And the supermarket video 'hits'
include lots of grainy black and white John Wayne shoot 'em ups,
some Technicolour Wayne, Robert Mitchum and Kirk Douglas
material and video packages of Eastwood's *Rawhide* adventures.

Fritz Manes says everybody loves cowboys. Well, it seems
the baby-boomers do and those flickering golden-gun carryings-
on are now being marketed as their own particular brand of cut-
price cartoons. It is a surprisingly successful substitution for the
normal dismal television network programming. Some years ago
TV-AM in Britain scored remarkable viewing figures when they
ran the campy sixties *Batman* television series. To the children
of Britain it was all brand new material.

If the Western is to have a big screen revival in the nineties –
they are doing television remakes of *Bonanza*, *The Rifleman* and

Gunsmoke in Hollywood – clearly Eastwood is the white knight in this particular business, the cowboy wielding shining six-guns. You only have to look again at *Josey Wales* to know that. It opens with him tilling honest soil on his Missouri farm as the American Civil War is ending. Then guerrilla raiders burst this particular bubble of tranquillity torching his home and killing his wife and child and he becomes the Outlaw Josey Wales. At a glance it seems the story of so many films all across the genres. But this tale had a remarkable genesis. It was written by half-Cherokee Forrest Carter, a self-taught Indian poet and storyteller. He was persuaded to sit down and write one of his stories and Whippoorwill Publishing in Arkansas printed the book. They published exactly seventy-five copies of *The Rebel Outlaw: Josey Wales*.

The book was sent to Eastwood's producer Bob Daley who found it moving *and* a page-turner. Unusually, he sent it from the office to Eastwood who was in Carmel. The company decision-maker also felt it 'had soul' and wanted to turn it into a film, in which Josey Wales loses one family but gains another, albeit a family of camp followers. Although the action is conventional the detail is realistic and there is much wry humour usually provided by Chief Dan George acting as the ageing, folk-lore overloaded, tough-as-old-boots Indian Chief Lone Watie.

Much of Eastwood's attitude to life – and death – is reflected in this film. The Civil War is shown as such a wanton waste of life. But the message is not sledge-hammered at the audience like some Oliver Stone film. Instead, you get Josey Wales muttering: 'Dyin' ain't much of a livin'.' And when Josey blows away a couple of bounty hunters his badly wounded saddle partner (Sam Bottoms) says: 'Wish we had time to bury them fellers.' Josey spits tobacco juice on the face of one corpse and says: 'To hell with them fellers. Buzzards got to eat, same as worms.'

Ah, the Wild West philosophy. Eastwood shoots a great line. And it is very useful punctuation in the trek across Texas around the army, the bounty hunters and the bad men who sell whiskey and women to the Indians. Sondra Locke is in the frame as lost Laura Lee who with her Grandma Sarah (Paula Trueman) completes Josey Wales' Mild Bunch. But although all around him might be nervy and frightened Eastwood's hero is never rattled. His is the invincible man of fiction. The gunplay is conventional and so is much of the a-man's-gotta-do-what-a-man's-gotta do packet psychology.

The twists are provided by Eastwood as director. Here we see the actor-director so frustrated by the lack of challenge during the *Rawhide* years (Eastwood: 'I called it 'Rawmeat'') trying to stretch the genre into the post-Vietnam and Richard Nixon seventies of America. Of course one must not dwell too much on the *auteur* aspects. One reviewer of a literary tome on Eastwood's motivations suggested that reading too much between the celluloid frames invited the reaction of the crowd to a blowhard in Mel Brook's *Blazing Saddles* when they chanted: 'Blow it up your arse, Harold.'

But nearly a decade after *The Outlaw Josey Wales* few critics were echoing that sort of sentiment towards Eastwood. He and Sondra Locke had enjoyed a very established and stable relationship. Curiously, as Eastwood the film-maker's career blossomed, Eastwood the lover-partner-companion's longterm Locke relationship wilted.

.   .   .

Professionally, Eastwood was on top in 1985. He had finally won respect as a serious artist. Privately, he and Sondra Locke were not the blissful couple they had once been and they would never work together again. And Maggie Eastwood was getting married again. Her former husband made it clear that if there ever was a wedding, he wouldn't be attending. He never got a chance – his ex-wife didn't tell him about it. Eastwood was fifty-five and very set in his ways, a man who needed things done his way. He was shaken by

Maggie Eastwood's decision to marry again. It was something he never thought would happen. Whether it was strictly subliminal or premeditated, he was encouraging Sondra Locke to get involved in projects he was not associated with to make herself independent of him.

'Of course, she gets Clint's pictures – she's his girlfriend.' Sondra Locke says it was comments like that that made her go it alone with *Ratboy*. Well, not exactly alone. When she decided to direct and star in the film – Rob Thompson's story about a woman who discovers a freaky, rat-like being she then tries to exploit – she needed a crew. Eastwood wasn't making a film at the time so she hired his: 'I could have hired people I didn't know, but the Malpaso crew I'd worked with for years and knew well. They're one of the best crews in the business, talented and fast,' she said before filming began.

She also said something which showed the heady aspirations one can get by being with such a major star as Eastwood:

I was looking for a good, challenging role for myself and I saw nothing there. Then I picked it up and reread it. There was something unique about the story. I just couldn't stop thinking about it. It haunted me – so much so that I decided: it may not be the role I'm looking for but why don't I direct it?

She approached Warner Brothers who distribute Eastwood's films and surprise, surprise, without much hesitation they agreed she could make the film. Eastwood stayed away from the project apart from watching some dailies (footage from a particular day's filming) of what Locke called 'a little fairy tale'.

Maggie Eastwood, meanwhile, was living out a Hawaiian fantasy. On 6 April 1985, she went through a sunset wedding ceremony on the lawns of the Mauna Kea Beach Hotel in Hawaii with Henry Wynberg who after the ceremony said: 'For Maggie and me there's no one else now. We're sure this is it – for the rest of our lives.'

His bride said: 'There's only one man in my life now and that's Henry. I just want to cry with happiness.' Brides and grooms say such things at weddings.

Kyle and Alison Eastwood were among the fifteen guests who wore flower leis for the ceremony – the newly-weds wore white orchid leis. Two of singer Paul Anka's daughters also attended the ceremony conducted by the Revd Walter Frutiger, a local minister. Wynberg, who lived with Elizabeth Taylor for fourteen months in 1974 and 1975, said he had not told her he was getting married. And Eastwood was kept in the dark too. 'They'll have to read about it in the newspapers,' he said with disdain. When he did, Clint Eastwood told friends the marriage wouldn't last. It didn't.

Eastwood himself by then was riding high on *Pale Rider* and his outing as the sexually twisted Wes Block in *Tightrope* had won critical raves. Early in 1985 there was even talk of an Oscar nomination for the role. He was more pragmatic than those touting his performance: 'I'm popular with the public but that doesn't make me popular at the country club.'

He called it right. No Oscar nomination. But his work was celebrated at the British Film Institute and he was the superstar of choice at the 1985 Cannes Film Festival where the ultimate status symbol remains the yacht. Eastwood was aboard the *Broke* that year, a yacht rented for him by Warner Brothers Studios. It was under 24-hour paparazzi watch. And starlet patrol. There were girls everywhere who would have been happy for Eastwood to make them stars if only for the night. Or day. Or afternoon.

His presence resulted in one of the biggest press conferences in the history of the Cannes Film Festival for *Pale Rider*. Some questions were rather bizarre. Was he, when he killed a bad guy in *Pale Rider*, in fact killing his father, Sergio Leone? Eastwood thought not but said everyone could have their opinion. There was reverence and indignation at the conference which was held in a hall five times larger than the normal press salon. 'Aren't there any good screenwriters left in Hollywood?,' asked one French journalist putting down what he called 'trite' dialogue in *Pale Rider*. Eastwood kept cool. Even if the Frenchman didn't like the film, he couldn't complain about the price – the press gets in free. Would he like to dedicate the film to anyone? 'Yes, I'll dedicate it to every person who's been missing a Western in recent years.'

Eastwood has God-like status in Europe, especially in France where he has become as revered as the late Steve McQueen. Other honours that year were a retrospective at the New York Museum of Modern Art, the Deauville Film Festival and the Montreal Film Festival. He was asked at Cannes about this sudden serious acceptance. 'I think a lot of people who are critics now came of age with my movies. Maybe they had a good experience with a girl at one of my movies and feel they owe me something.'

But Eastwood also had detractors – especially now that he was being taken seriously. He also has a tremendous memory and has never forgotten slights against him from even his earliest days in Hollywood. Which is why those who talk against him shoot him in the back, as it were. He would make better films if he worked with better writers, actors and directors, say some. 'He doesn't like to share the screen with a powerful, name actress; or submit himself to be directed by a big name director,' said one producer. 'He's cheap. He's won't normally pay more than $50,000 for a script which is a tenth of the going rate,' said one successful Hollywood writer.

Eastwood sat on a couch in his office at Burbank Studios and listened to the remarks by his detractors who naturally wanted to remain anonymous. On the scripts he said: 'That's not true. If it's a good screenplay, I'll pay for it. But I'm not going to hire somebody just because he's got a great name. Even the most expensive guys turn out crap.'

On big name co-stars: 'This is one thing that does bother me about the business here and in New York. Everybody's after the same actors of the moment. Nobody comes up with Carrie Snodgress [*Pale Rider*] or Jessica Walter [*Play Misty for Me*] and Sondra wasn't exactly running with activity when I used her in *The Outlaw Josey Wales*. The point is there are dozens of fine actresses out there who are as talented – and some more talented – than Jessica Lange or Sally Field or Sissy Spacek. But these other actresses are not the gals of the moment – the fad of the moment – so nobody hires them.

'This is what really drags me about the business. I hate the way they discard people, particularly the women. One minute they're given all the praise and the next minute they're dustmops. It's a real shame. So, I've tried to use good people who maybe don't have the big names of, say, a Jessica Lange.

'None of these so-called hot actresses is a heavy-leaguer like Vivien Leigh but they're gals of the moment and two years from now there'll be others. I just don't see the reason to work with them. It's not just money that's stopped me. I've paid some big money to actresses – Genevieve Bujold in *Tightrope*, for example. My flashpoint is just the inequities of the business. You've got the Golden Globe crowd who don't know a thing about acting and who don't even try to learn. And then you've got the Academy Awards group which is more political and so often gives Oscars to actors who don't have popular appeal and therefore aren't threatening – people like F. Murray Abraham or Ben Kingsley. I'm not putting these people down. I'm just saying that a popular movie star like Paul Newman doesn't have a chance against them.

'So, I'm inclined towards the underdog. I guess I've always been rebellious in that way. I think it had to do with how I was raised. My father used to say to me: "Show 'em what you can do and don't worry about what you're gonna get. Say you'll work for free and make yourself invaluable." That approach builds your confidence. If I hadn't been brought up that way I might have reacted differently to the criticism received early on in my career in the terms of contents of my films – *Dirty Harry* being called a fascist is one of many examples. I might have said to myself: "Well, I've had some success, I'll do something a little more middle-of-the-road and not offend anybody." But by not offending anybody, you do offend somebody – yourself.'

SIX

Gung-ho

'Some people think that when you're older you're supposed to sit down and watch TV reruns and squeeze beer cans. That isn't for me.'

CLINT EASTWOOD ON AGEING

Patt Morrison is a reporter for the *Los Angeles Times* newspaper. She is clever, witty and always wears a hat. If any member of the British Royal Family is visiting California, she will be on the trail having bought a new hat for the occasion. In fact, she buys a hat for all important events. She says she can't recall what hat she wore in August 1985, when she flew up to Carmel from Los Angeles to write a story about one of California's most popular tourist resorts. The story was perfect for her because it involved an absurd situation – and she's excellent at deriding pomposity and deflating egos.

The essence of her story that summer in the *Times* was that the City Fathers of Carmel were going all out to stop the selling of ice-cream cones. Some people thought that snacking in the street even in hot weather was undignified. Ms Morrison thought that stupid. And said so. The headline on the story shouted 'SCROOGE CITY' and told how the Council denied a businessman a permit to sell ice-cream cones using an ordinance forbidding take-out food. But there were also the laws banning children from the parks, frisbees and drivers stopping to watch the sunsets. Eastwood was not amused about what he regarded as a negative image being broadcast across America – the newspaper wire services picked up the story – about the town he loves. He did not regard the incumbents at City Hall with the same sentiment. In fact, he'd just about had-it-up-to-here with them.

And so, Patt Morrison became responsible for Clint Eastwood going into politics and becoming a candidate for Mayor of Carmel, Hizzoner, the boss of the five-member council and eighteen-strong police force.

After his separation from Maggie Eastwood, he had built a new home two miles from Carmel, a high-tech stone house, with a private beach, overlooking the Pacific. It was his Carmel Castle, home in the area he had fallen instantly in love with years before. There is a six-foot-high fence with nails on top to discourage racoons around the property. By 1985 he had lived in the area proper for nearly fourteen years. Both his children went to American public (that is, not private) schools in the area. He had made financial contributions to town charities, specifically the Sunset Cultural Center and continues to do so. When you walk through Carmel with him he is so low-key that there is hardly a glance. If a group of tourists spots him, it is a different matter – stares and cameras clicking. But in his sports jackets and jeans, maybe a windcheater on a chilly evening, he does not advertise his fame. He'll most likely drive into town in his pick-up truck. Giuliano's is one of his favoured restaurants and Susan Negri who runs it says:

When he comes in for dinner, the women all seem to want more coffee. But he never pushes. When he arrives without a reservation, he'll wait for a table just like anyone else – often he'll come back later rather than cause a stir.

But in 1985, he stirred things up. Quaint, style-conscious Carmel with no street numbers and no cemetery appropriately got the Man With No Name to deal with. Eastwood – 'I'm no property developer' – had plans to build a two-storey office building next to his popular restaurant the Hog's Breath Inn. George Brook-Kothlow, the architect who designed the building – and Eastwood's former home where Maggie Eastwood now lives – said the city 'never offered any clear-cut direction to what they were having a problem with.' Eastwood's next-door-neighbour is Russ Harris and he remembered:

It's one thing to maintain the charm of the community but what really riled up Clint was that their decision seemed totally arbitrary. What really irked him is if that was happening to him, what was happening to the little guy in town?

This is what happened then: regulations designed to keep business in the background obstruct all development despite the fact that the city's budget ($6 million in 1985/6) operates from such revenue. Property taxes are small. The 1929 city charter is clear that Carmel belongs to the people who live there and business is 'subordinate to its residential character'. All shop signs needed approval and any outside design changes. If you wanted to put in a skylight or paint the front door, just make an appointment with the Planning Commission.

The city said Eastwood's proposed building would be too close to the sidewalk. They said the exterior contained too much glass and not enough wood. Eastwood and partner, Maggie Eastwood, with whom he continued a business relationship, sued the city saying the regulations were 'vague, subjective, ambiguous, unintelligible and obscure'. In November 1985, the two sides settled out of court. Eastwood could build but to modified plans. He was not happy. There was a new glint in his eye. Dirty Harry and some of his other screen characters have tended to get ticked off about bureaucracy and take the law into their own hands. Eastwood considered becoming the law.

'We all knew he was frustrated,' said George Brook-Kothlow adding, 'but there was no indication he'd personally get involved other than to support a new candidate with a more viable point of view with respect to commercial versus residential interests.'

As the new election year approached, Eastwood, not rushing in like a fool, commissioned a telephone poll to see if the residents of Carmel wanted a new mayor and if they wanted him in the $200 a month job – a position of little money and lots of aggravation. What the poll showed was there was no great support for the current administration of Mayor Charlotte Townsend who was then sixty-one, an earnest, friendly and sincere 'local neighbourhood lady'. But a lady who liked the neighbourhood the way it was.

In the summer of 1985 Eastwood was asked point blank by *Rolling Stone* magazine if he would ever run for political office and he replied: 'That's something nobody has to worry about.' That all changed at 4:20 p.m. on 30 January 1986. Before the 5 p.m. deadline that day Eastwood arrived fresh from the opening round of the Pebble Beach National Pro-Am golf tournament and dropped off his nominating petition for mayor. It was endorsed by thirty – ten more than needed – registered voters. Ronald Reagan, former actor, was in the White House. Clint Eastwood, actor, producer, director and one of the world's most popular cinema attractions wanted to be in Carmel City Hall.

'I don't need to bring attention to myself,' he told Carmel's weekly newspaper the *Pine Cone* in his first interview as a candidate – also the paper's first world exclusive – adamantly going on: 'I'm doing this as a resident. This is where I live; this is where I intend to live the rest of my life. I have a great affinity with this community. There used to be a great deal of camaraderie, a great spirit in this community. Now there is such negativity. I'd like to see the old spirit come back here, that kind of *esprit de corps*.'

Every morning Eastwood runs several miles as part of his daily work-out. Now he was running for something altogether different. But still, he argued, for his own well-being.

Eastwood was stumping for less government intervention. He wanted to do something about the problem of tourist parking. He decried restrictive zoning laws. He was particularly hot on the ice-cream-cone issue. 'I can recall a time when you could walk down the street in Carmel and pick up an ice-cream cone at a shop – now you'd be fined.'

For those who wondered about being mayor and being a movie star, Eastwood who had taken off most of 1985 – he said 'personal reasons' when asked during the campaign – to spend more time and try and have more influence over his two teenage children promised: 'The city will be my absolute priority. I'll be a lot less active in films than I have in the past.' He went on the campaign trail. Usually his politician's outfit was a tweed sports jacket, grey slacks and shirt and tie. He went on the tea and biscuits circuit. He attended the Monterey Bay Republican Ladies Club. He went anywhere he could to get a vote. He kissed babies. He shook hands. He refused autographs, but with a polite: 'Thanks for asking.'

Eastwood said more in one day on the campaign trail than he had in thirty movies. He was gushing as Zsa Zsa Gabor the day I went with him to the Kiwanis Club (a Rotary Club type organization). Of course, the campaign didn't just interest the residents of Carmel. There were media from all over the world. At the Kiwanis Club a pushy and apparently not requested aide wondered what a Japanese film crew wanted to know about Carmel. 'Nothing . . . but in my country, Mr Eastwood is biggest star,' came the reply. Eastwood overheard this. He arranged his rangy 6ft 4ins frame to find the film crew's level and did the interview.

Today Carmel, tomorrow Washington? It was a question time and time again. He was diplomatic: 'I've been there four times. The last time Nancy Reagan called up and said Prince Charles and Princess Diana are coming and they want to meet you. There will be eighty people. I said: "That's very nice, count me as one."' Political ambitions? 'Ronald Reagan can get on with running the country. The fact we have construction-site toilets behind the Pine Inn is really disgraceful.'

It was only outsiders who considered Eastwood a sure thing at the 8 April 1986 election. But his celebrity was no assurance of that. The town is used to famous faces and residents include Doris Day, Paul Anka and Joan Fontaine; what Eastwood had to do was convince the town that his politics were not some whim and he was not a fluke. The message he gave to town meetings was straightforward: 'I hope the voters of Carmel base their decision on election day not on my career as an actor and producer but on my involvement in this community and my experience and desire to be a good mayor. This is between my neighbours and me.'

The ballot on 8 April was probably the most intensely scrutinized small-town election in American history. Eastwood received 2166 votes – 72 per cent of the total – easily to defeat incumbent and former librarian Charlotte Townsend. 'I would like to think we can now take the community out of the hands of the few and put it in the hands of the many, the people of Carmel,' he said in his victory speech. Later, he was asked if he wanted to be known as Mr Mayor and replied: 'Nah, just Clint.'

Eastwood had cast his own vote at All Saints Episcopal Church having arrived in his old pale-yellow Volkswagen convertible. The event was treated like something from a presidential election – the candidates were outnumbered 50-1 by the media – and there was a curious ballet as photographers jostled for the best camera angles. It was like Cannes without the starlets.

A day after his victory, Mayor Eastwood was meeting with friends to discuss the election and future moves. A telephone call interrupted the meeting. The caller asked Eastwood: 'What's an actor who once appeared with a monkey in a movie doing in politics?' President Ronald Reagan, who was an actor in 1951 and made *Bedtime for Bonzo* with a chimpanzee co-star, was on the line from Washington. Eastwood, who co-starred with Clyde the orang-utan in two films, assured the president that his political ambitions ended at the Carmel city limit.

'He used my line, "Make my day" so I borrowed his "Get government off my back,"' said the mayor. James Stewart who appeared in Eastwood's favourite film *Mr Smith Goes to Washington* also telephoned congratulations.

Eastwood decided not to retire from film-making for all of his two-year term as mayor. He had found the ten-week campaign tiring. Clearly, he would rather have been making movies than drinking weak tea and attending fifty-five coffee mornings. But he was happy to have won. A week later, dressed in a grey suit and red tie, he was sworn in as mayor. His mother was there. And so was his sister, and Charlotte Townsend handed over the gavel to him. As he again said his priority would now be Carmel and not the movies you could almost hear the groans in the corporate offices of Hollywood.

On 6 May, at his first council meeting, Eastwood dealt with an agenda of fifty items keeping his promise to get on with the job. He also took revenge on some of his opponents. He sacked four planning commissioners who had turned down his plans to build the office next to the Hog's Breath Inn. Don't get mad, get even. Within two months of him being in office, there were more changes in Carmel than in the previous ten years. Ice-cream cones were on sale, a new car park had been built, steps to the beaches were under repair, more public toilets had been installed, ramps for the handicapped constructed and a new pedestrian bridge erected. The next move was to lift the ordinance banning high-heeled shoes.

But any frivolity was suddenly lost when Eastwood election campaign worker David Archer, then forty-two, was arrested for rape and murder. Archer was caught after being chased by police down the Pacific Coast Highway. Eastwood said 200 volunteers had helped him in the campaign and Archer was simply one of them. Archer, charged in Carmel with killing a repair man during a robbery and raping a woman at a party to celebrate Eastwood's election, maintained he was very close to the mayor. He said he would call Eastwood to testify at his trial. He never did.

And Eastwood returned to more mundane matters of local government. He could be found in someone else's garage trying to decide whether it could be moved three inches north. A typical day started with meetings at City Hall at 9 a.m., a tour of the town – on foot – and then budget or planning-commission conferences. Evening council meetings often ran six hours and sometimes past midnight. On the longtime Eastwood movie policy of less talking the more action, he limited speeches to three minutes.

Eastwood, as promised, did make being mayor of Carmel his priority. However, he still managed to make two films during his two-year term. One was *Bird* the story of jazz great Charlie Parker which he produced and directed. The other was *Heartbreak Ridge* which he produced, directed and starred in. And which got Hizzoner in hot water with the US Marine Corps.

. . .

While Mayor Eastwood was taking control in Carmel, first-time director Sondra Locke had completed filming *Ratboy*. It opened in American cinemas in the summer of 1986 but turned off the critics and didn't turn on any audiences. Locke was philosophical about it. She was also impressed by Eastwood's election which she called the 'idealistic gesture' on his behalf.

For the movies, Eastwood himself was preparing a crowd-pleaser with *Heartbreak Ridge*. It was fun if formula stuff. He would star as Gunnery Sergeant Tom Highway who had to knock an inexperienced grab-bag of sloppy marines into shape during the invasion of Grenada in 1983. Of course, he could drink, fight and curse better than anyone else in the marines: Eastwood meets *The Dirty Dozen*. Except he was too dirty. The US Defense Department gave their full co-operation before filming began, but after screening of the film on 14 November 1986, they objected to 'an excessive amount of profanity'. They then withdrew support for the film which led to the cancellations of benefit screenings for the marines and tributes to them being scrapped from the film's credits – an enormous publicity boost for *Heartbreak Ridge*.

In the film Eastwood plays quintessential Eastwood. A man of straightforward principles, he likes nothing better than a fight or a drink or vice versa. A special unofficial screening was set up for members of the Marine Corps who liked the film, Eastwood's old-fashioned stereotype character, and thought the language was realistic. But officially, the Corps completely distanced themselves from the film.

Eastwood was in Carmel chairing a city council meeting when the flap started. Typically, he found the bureaucratic reaction silly. 'It's a shame that a charity has to lose money because of somebody who's got a bee under his rear end somewhere. It's not something of national security. In the words of Alfred Hitchcock, "It's just a movie."'

Marine Corps official Lt Colonel John Shotwell said the whole tone of the film was objectionable. Especially one scene where Eastwood as Sgt Highway pumps an extra round of ammunition into the back of a Cuban soldier he has already shot. Eastwood said that in combat, marines occasionally do make sure the enemy is dead. He got quite irritated by the fuss, although admitted the script took some liberties and that he ignored the other services involved in the Grenada invasion: 'There were a lot of people there. We were showing twelve guys, a small reconnaissance platoon. What am I supposed to do, spend another $5 million showing the army's invasion? It's insane.'

Eastwood, again typically, counterattacked. In the original script, Sgt Highway's squad is rerouted to Grenada while on their way to Beirut to replace marines killed during the terrorist bombing in 1983. That is, in fact, how some marines got to Grenada. The Department of Defense wanted no mention of that and Eastwood eventually agreed to take it out of his film. 'They didn't want to acknowledge that incident and that's sort of altering history. I'm sure relatives of people killed in Beirut wouldn't like having that history denied.'

Government co-operation for film-makers is a balancing act. The film people get access to military bases and equipment and the Services get Technicolour recruitment advertisements. The navy was turning away recruits after Richard Gere's role in *An Officer and a Gentleman* which was made without its co-operation and

Tom Cruise's *Top Gun* which was made with it. Even when John Wayne's 1949 the *Sands of Iwo Jima* is shown on television, marine recruitment gets a boost. Ironically, there is a scene in *Iwo* which might appear more harmful to the marines than *Heartbreak Ridge*. Wayne's Sgt Stryker, angry with a recruit who falls over himself during a bayonet training, intentionally slams him in the jaw with a rifle butt. That is a court-martial offence, was then, is now, but the marine command in Washington approved all of this film.

'It was the only scene I objected to,' said retired Brig. Gen. Leonard Freibourg, who was a major representing the marines on the filming of *Iwo*. 'I went to DC with it and the answer came back the next day. DC said, "Tone down the severity of the blow, but let it go. It's a good story point."' The butting incident seems to be there to set up a comic-relief scene a few minutes later, where Sgt Stryker shows the clumsy recruit how to get into the bayonet rhythm by doing the Mexican hat dance with him. The closest that *Heartbreak Ridge* comes to that brutality happens when Eastwood rips an earring off one of his troops, and it, too, is played for laughs.

Retired Col. George Gilliland, who talked Darryl F. Zanuck into making *The Halls of Montezuma* at Twentieth Century Fox in 1950 and served as the marine liaison officer during the filming, said that the entire Marine Corps command wanted to help write the script. Gilliland himself objected to the casting of Richard Widmark in the starring role, because he had pushed an old lady in a wheelchair down a flight of stairs in 1947's *Kiss of Death*. Widmark got the part anyway, and Gilliland said once the film was under way, there was no conflict between the government and director Lewis Milestone. But occasionally he had to fight for moments of authenticity. He says:

> *They had one scene where a grenade goes off and ten guys jump into the hole it left. I said, 'Grenades don't leave holes.' They said, 'Well, they did in* For Whom the Bell Tolls. *I said, 'Well, now there are ten million men who know better.'*

Mario Van Peebles who co-starred as a wise-guy recruit in *Heartbreak Ridge* said that no one expected any problems with the Marine Corps. Although he had one when he reported for filming on location at Camp Pendleton about fifty miles north of San Diego, California. The drill instructor thought he was a new recruit:

The first one yelled: 'Motherfucker, get down now and give me fifty push-ups. Now!' Then another instructor looked at me and said: 'Don't go eyeballing the sergeant, boy! Git down!' I did the push-ups. I felt it was in my best interest.

Peebles, who appears regularly on the *LA Law* television series, was handpicked by Eastwood for *Heartbreak Ridge*. The male model turned actor was born in Mexico City and taken around the world by his composer-writer father, Melvin Van Peebles. Eastwood, again, had recognized talent others seemed to have overlooked: 'Clint instilled a gung-ho attitude in me. He told me to be all I could be. We got to be pals. He even let me write three songs for the movie.' It's another example of Eastwood going that little bit further for people. He genuinely seems to want to help, maybe to pay a little back for his own good fortune. And, of course, there is his memory.

Actress Marsha Mason had been set to co-star with Eastwood and Burt Reynolds in *City Heat* in 1984 but after rewrites she felt the role wasn't her:

I really hated to leave the project. I felt badly about it but my character was so different – actually it became a completely different movie and I couldn't connect with it anymore. Clint was wonderful about it.

He's extremely down to earth, very unspoiled, very modest. He's certainly not Dirty Harry – there's none of that character's intensity, wariness or sense of menace.

And when Sgt Tom Highway needed an ex-wife in *Heartbreak Ridge* it was Marsha Mason who got the call. As Aggie, now a waitress who has waited through the Korean and Vietnam wars for her man, she was the one who got to play with softy Eastwood. Mason said:

He married this young thing and then went off carousing with all the other ladies. Now he's trying to figure out how to get Aggie back so he's reading the women's magazines. 'Did we have a meaningful relationship,' he asks me. He's in kind of a crisis.

Eastwood agrees with that. And says that's what drew him to the character. The actor himself was being drawn in many directions at the time. He was concerned about fulfilling his job as mayor, about his children, about Sondra Locke – Eastwood was trying to juggle all the balls in the air which makes it even more interesting when he talks about his Sgt Highway.

'It's about love, really. Not only between Tom Highway and his ex-wife, but among friends, people, fellow mankind. That sort of thing, that's the subtext of it. Highway is a man at a crossroads, in life and in his career. He's approaching mandatory retirement, and he's trying to come to terms with the world he'll be facing after the service. He's been a problem soldier, too. He's a brawler. He drinks too much. By this time, he probably should have been promoted to the maximum rank. Especially being a Congressional Medal of Honor winner. But he's a little bit of a screw-up.

'Highway sort of represents the old military, as opposed to the new military – the "Be all you can be" recruiting slogan, or "It's not just a job, it's an adventure," or "The marines are looking for a few good men." All that kind of stuff where guys work on computers and seem to be having a good time. But he's from the old infantry school. He's scarred up. He's a fighter, and none of that new stuff makes sense to him.

'He's never really understood women at all. He's been with a lot of women, but now he's trying to get a handle on it through his relationship with his ex-wife, which he would like to get sorted out. But she just throws it back at him in a very honest way: "The only reason you want to get together now is because it's all coming to an end." So he's sort of a lost soul, an empty soul. Sort of a guy who's very hard-boiled, but at the same time searching for the sensitivities of his own soul.

'I think, he's like a lot of men. There's a lot of very macho guys who are that way, because they don't realize there's something else there. They've matured in some ways but not in others. But there often comes a point where you look back and realize that you don't know a lot. Highway's that kind of guy, and that's what appealed to me. That and the fact that it wasn't an action film. I've done a lot of those, and they're fine, but here we're looking for characters with other elements to them. If you've been around as long as I have, they'll let you do that.'

.   .   .

There were those who said the voters and residents of Carmel were indulging Eastwood in his role as mayor. That may or may not have been the case. But it is a fact that Hollywood studios were willing – and would have been betraying their stockholders if they hadn't – to indulge a star with such a box-office record.

Eastwood persuaded Warner Brothers to get the script of *Bird* for him from Columbia Pictures in a behind-the-scenes deal whereby Warners gave Columbia a film called *Revenge* which was perceived as a strong commercial property by legendary producer Ray Stark. (Ironically, it would be an unusual thing, a Kevin Costner flop some years later.) At first Stark, one of the most canny of Hollywood moguls and one of the few major deal-makers left from the Golden Age, was suspicious. He thought Warner wanted the *Bird* script for Prince who had had a huge success with *Purple Rain*. When he was told it was for Eastwood he laughed: 'What, Clint Eastwood playing Charlie Parker?' Nevertheless, Eastwood was displaying clout, as Sondra Locke would say, to the nth degree and the script switch went ahead. When the negotiations were over, Eastwood was like a little boy. Clearly, it was never a commercial project. But for every *Bird* in the hand were there not two *Dirty Harrys* in the bush?

A long film, two hours and forty-three minutes, it is also dark. Whatever demons drove Charlie Bird Parker, a saxophonist of genius and a pioneer of modern jazz, to such creative heights and depths of dissolution and destruction in 1955? A film about a man drinking and drugging himself to death at thirty-four? Ah, but it's a jazzman killing himself. And Eastwood is a jazz fanatic. Nevertheless, the story of Bird was not uplifting. When he died watching television, the examining doctor estimated his age at sixty. *Bird* is a harrowing story – a film made in purgatorial darkness.

Parker – he was called Bird after the nickname Yardbird he was given in Kansas City where he ate a lot of chicken while hanging around the Reno Club, a meeting place for jazz musicians – had fascinated Eastwood for years. He had been following the resurgence in traditional jazz – Lu Watters, Bob Scobey and Kid Ory – but then first heard Parker play when he was living in Oakland. He didn't understand him initially, but it got him very interested.

His mother was a Fats Waller fan. At fifteen, Eastwood could play the piano well enough to perform at the Omar Club on Broadway in Oakland. The regulations were slack – the teenaged Eastwood played for free meals. He was still at school and the only instrument available was the flugelhorn. It wasn't considered very hip. Eastwood played it anyway. But he concentrated on ragtime and blues piano and he can be heard, years later, at the piano along with Mike Lang and Pete Jolly as part of a three-keyboard boogie-woogie number on the soundtrack album of *City Heat*.

Eastwood followed Dave Brubeck, Coleman Hawkins, Howard McGhee and Hank Jones. When he was in the army at Fort Ord, he heard Gerry Mulligan and Chet Baker, and in the army he also met Lennie Niehaus a former saxophone player with Stan Kenton. Eastwood's memory . . . Niehaus wrote the music for *Tightrope*, *City Heat*, *Pale Rider*, *Heartbreak Ridge*, and when *Bird* flew into the pictures, he had to bring out his saxophone again. It was his job to teach Forest Whitaker who had the title role how to play. Niehaus says Eastwood's personality has not changed over the years: 'He was sweet tempered when I knew him in the army and he's the same gentle man now. You never hear him yell.'

He can, however, put the knife in. During the filming of *Bird* he would regularly be back and forth to Carmel to take care of council business. British producer David Puttnam, who was then head of Columbia Studios, had complained that executives had to work weekends – a complaint which had seemed risible to most of Hollywood. And to Eastwood: 'If David Puttnam really wants to give up his Sundays, let him try being mayor of a small town.' Of course, it was Eastwood's choice to juggle politics and film-making.

Yet why another film about a druggie jazz musician. 'Charlie Parker was a guy who was ahead of his time,' says Eastwood, adding: 'He was one of those people influential in forming the last major harmonic change in music. He was a drug user, but he put down people like himself who used them.' Eastwood says he did not want to shove any anti-drug message down audiences' throats. He wanted to present the story and have people make their own decisions. He has never smoked except on film and has never experimented with drugs. He says of his growing-up days: 'We sort of lived by the saying; "If there's anything better than a woman and a cold beer you better not tell me about it. It might kill me."'

Bird was only the second film Eastwood directed in which he did not appear – and where he 'could dress like a bum, my usual fashion'; the other was *Breezy* in 1973. In that film, the late William

Holden is the older businessman involved with Kay Lenz's California blonde Breezy who is years younger. The rumour at the time was that Eastwood was attracted to the script because he was involved in a similar situation. Sondra Locke, of course, had auditioned for the role of Breezy.

William Holden didn't care about that. During filming he was still marvelling over Eastwood's powers of persuasion. Holden, who died after a fall at his apartment in Santa Monica in 1980, had enjoyed a remarkable career – films like *Stalag 17* and *The Bridge on the River Kwai* – for more than three decades when he agreed to star in *Breezy*. He thought he knew all about Hollywood and deal-making yet he worked for Eastwood for no salary and, instead received a percentage of the profits. Sadly, for Holden, the film was not a great hit. In fact, the American actors' union, the Screen Actors' Guild (SAG), contacted Eastwood six months after the film was released and told him that just to keep things proper he had to pay Holden $4000 – minimum SAG wages – to keep within union rules.

Eastwood makes his own rules while filming. Tom Stern has been the chief lighting technician on eight of Eastwood's movies:

> *He's so fast because he has all of us pulling for him. I have the lowest seniority of the core group. His wardrobe man has been with him since 1959. Clint's not particularly verbal. He talks with his hands so you flounder for a while and it took me a picture and a half to understand him. He's completely committed to his intuition.*

And he keeps things cool according to longtime executive producer David Valdes: 'Tempers never flare, you're never walking on eggshells. On a lot of sets there is always panic, but not with him.'

While he was filming *Bird* there was a move to get him into national politics. The presidency of Ronald Reagan was in its final reel in 1987–8 and after the Gipper why not Dirty Harry? In

Carmel they were selling 'Clint Eastwood for President' T-shirts for $12.95. Eastwood's fans claimed he was more macho than George Bush, more conservative than Robert Dole, another presidential candidate. 'Based on name identification alone, he would be a viable national or state-wide candidate,' said Senator John Seymour, chairman of the California Republican Caucus, trying to enlist Eastwood. 'He looks good, he sounds good and he can do what none of the other famous hot dogs can do – say he started at the grass roots.'

And that's what they were in Carmel. During one Council debate, an interminable series of speeches, over whether a Stop or Slow sign should be erected at a busy intersection the mayor observed: 'With a Stop sign at least they'll slow down after they've gone through it.'

Eastwood enjoyed the council meetings. There were some offbeat moments. Twice a thirtysomething blonde stood up at meetings and pledged her undying love to him and asked him to marry her. The second time he quietly told her: 'I tried marriage once, ma'am, and it didn't work.'

Politicians are always being accused of throwing money at problems they can't cope with. They use taxpayer's money. Eastwood used his own to stop a development project to build town houses on the 22-acre Mission Ranch on the southern edge of Carmel. He paid more than $5 million for the property which remains home to migrating birds, sheep, cows, residents and tourists who visit the Mission's restaurant and Old West saloon.

Yet despite his cool and potent public face, there is much internal churning for Eastwood. He keeps things to himself. On the surface, there is no problem – but? He tells one story of the night before he was about to make his début as a director with *Play Misty for Me*. He was in bed thinking through the movie, scene by scene, and how he would film each one. He says he felt uneasy because he was convinced he had forgotten something. What had slipped his mind was that he was also starring in the film. He switched on the light, picked up the script and started memorizing his lines.

Internal and external man. There are also two Eastwoods in Hollywood. There is the producer/director of films like *Bird*, the influence-maker who urged Warner Brothers to make the Oscar nominated *Round Midnight*, director Bertrand Tavernier's homage to American jazz in Paris. And there is the cool cowboy or cop who attracts giant audiences – he's the one the accountants love. But over his career for every outing as Dirty Harry or commercial venture like *Heartbreak Ridge*, there has been something for himself. Which was why he ran for mayor of Carmel and not president of the United States.

—

SEVEN

White Hat, Grey Heart

'The less we know about someone, the more we are apt to believe he is all we would like him to be.'

PSYCHIATRIST DR STANLEY PLATMAN ON THE EASTWOOD FACTOR

Clint Eastwood had no plans to go into national politics and despite massive support he decided early in 1988 not to run again for mayor. Instead he spent his last few hours in office bracing a wet chill swirling off San Francisco Bay as helicopters chattered overhead – Dirty Harry Callahan was back for the fifth time in *Dead Pool*. People whose names appeared on gambling lists were turning up dead and Harry was set loose to investigate. This was one for the box office – *Sudden Impact* five years earlier had earned more than $150 million.

The accountants were happy. Eastwood was editing *Bird* – it had very limited time in cinemas in America and only earned $2.2 million at the box office but won ovations at the Cannes Film Festival and world-wide critical plaudits – while filming *Dead Pool*. He said he wanted to see how Harry was coping 'at this stage of his life'.

Eastwood himself was at a professional crossroads. Other stars of his generation – Paul Newman, Warren Beatty, and Robert Redford – had been maintaining a lower profile producing or directing rather than starring. The austere *Wall Street Journal* had wondered in print if he wasn't getting a little long in the tooth to be still running around in shoot 'em ups. Eastwood wondered aloud if the *Journal* wasn't slowing up a little itself having, he thought, lost a lot of its zip. Dirty Harry had all the zip needed to turn a gang of thugs who interrupt his meal in a Chinese restaurant into Chow Mein in *The Dead Pool*. Too old? Getouttahere!

For years Eastwood has followed the advice of Durk Pearson and Sandy Shaw, the husband-and-wife authors of the Life Extension books. Nearly sixty, he said he felt better than at forty. The regime was the same in 1992 – a three mile jog, two hours in the gym and meditation twice a day – all of that every day. He maintains his low-fat, high vegetable, no red-meat diet except for the occasional hamburger. He takes choline selenium in yeast to feel more alert, deanol for verbal ability, L-arginine and L-dopa to help him exercise and other vitamin supplements for his skin. He golfs, he skis, he swims and frowns when you raise an eyebrow: 'Sex can be overrated.' In his early sixties he is fabulously fit and you almost have to run to keep up with his loping strides when he takes off around Carmel or across the Warner Brothers studio lot in Burbank.

He needs reading glasses and wore them for the last Carmel City Council meeting he presided over on 5 April 1988. 'I think he gave a freshness to the town – I'm a little annoyed he didn't decide to run again,' said aptly named restaurant owner Kate Curry that day. But seven others stepped in to try and replace him including divorcee and mother of three Jean Grace. Eastwood decided to support her in the election. Sondra Locke was then living mostly in Los Angeles – she would be seen at public functions with Eastwood but rarely in Carmel – and Mrs Grace admitted after lots of romantic gossip: 'I'm very fond of Clint. We go to parties. We go to dinners.' Eastwood has never commented on how political or romantic his relationship with Mrs Grace who replaced him as mayor was.

He would talk, though, about his two years in charge of the cosy, fifty-seat chamber: 'I've enjoyed it. It's been very challenging. The nature of the process isn't as effective as the private sector but you try and move efficiently through the process and include everyone and all their input. My celebrity may have hindered in the sense that a lot of times people would want you for appearances here and there that really had not much bearing on city business.

'Trying to juggle film and being mayor? Sometimes I said to myself: "What sort of merry-go-round is this?"' But it wasn't the workload that stopped him trying to be elected again: 'I have to take care of the personal stuff for awhile,' he said, adding pointedly: 'If you miss time with your family you wonder if it's retrievable time. Sometimes it isn't.' The decision made at the last minute was for himself and his children – Kyle was nineteen and

Alison aged fifteen. 'Formative years,' said their father indicating that if they had been older his decision might have been different.

The verdict on his tenure as mayor was largely favourable. He won praise for increasing the number of public toilets in town, improving facilities on the beach, breaking a long impasse over the expansion of the library and getting a greater share of water from a local dam. And Eastwood was still taking a major share of the movie action. As he filmed *Dead Pool* he was already planning to star in *Pink Cadillac* and preparing for *White Hunter, Black Heart* to film on location in Africa in 1990. He didn't seem to want to be at home. But he was still enamoured of Dirty Harry and said on location of his fifth outing as the loose cannon San Francisco cop: 'It's like revisiting someone you haven't seen for eighteen years. You figure: "I'll go back and see how he feels about things now. How is he existing eighteen years later?" All Dirty Harry has ever wanted is to make some sense of the system.

'Originally, the part was written for an older man than I was when I first played it. He was a guy who had been on the force a long time, a mature guy who was fed up with what he saw happening to people. The laws are crazy, he was saying. A lot of people felt that way. That's one reason the films are so popular.' The role of Inspector Harry Callahan had been turned down by John Wayne and Frank Sinatra before Eastwood pinned on San Francisco Police Department Badge 2211.

The *Dead Pool* although not as financially successful as *Sudden Impact* was another money-maker earning more than $80 million. The reason, according to psychiatrist Stanley Platman, that these films attract both men and women. He says:

It's the Clint Eastwood style of manhood that most people admire. He is not only a movie phenomenon but an 'ideal man' – the kind of man that men would like to be and the type that most women fantasize having a relationship with. People are always hungry for manly men. His give 'em hell approach is a refreshing change from what they see around them. It may be 'with it' to say that men should be free to express feelings but inwardly many people consider the man who shows his pains and problems as a 'softy'.

Both men and women find the hard-hitting, take charge, action-orientated man very appealing and admirably suited to our times. They don't really consider the Clint Eastwood style of punch 'em out manhood a thing of the past. Men see him as a buddy, a 'stand-up' guy who's loyal and unswerving. And women see him as an ideal protector, the man they'd like to have on their side when they cross a dark parking lot.

Dr Platman, former clinical Professor of Psychiatry at the University of Maryland, goes on:

Almost everyone knows someone they'd like to take a swing at – a neighbour, boss or relative who drives them up the wall. Eastwood handles that sort of frustration the way we'd like to but can't. He serves as our personal 'hit man'. And he has this extraordinary independence. He does his own thing and bows to no one. Every role he's played – cowboy, pilot, detective – heightens his image as a loner. He is the supreme example of the man who has made his own rules and made them work for him. He represents our most prized fantasy – to be totally independent and self-sufficient. And he doesn't water down his appeal by overexposure. The less we know about someone, the more apt we are to believe he is all we would like him to be.

Maggie Eastwood was finding out that Henry Wynberg was not at all what she wanted him to be. Her marriage, her children growing into far more aware late teenaged years were putting pressure on her – and on her former husband. With Wynberg there had been squabbles over his spending and his drinking. There were also rumours of other women. What had seemed an idyllic match during that Hawaiian ceremony had now collapsed into bickering and suspicion. Maggie Eastwood had talked to her former husband about it. They had 'family' conferences about it.

One was in London in August 1989. They giggled about reports that Eastwood was dating Jane Brolin the former wife of actor James Brolin. They had in fact been family friends for years and legendary Hollywood divorce lawyer Marvin Mitchelson confirmed: 'It was Clint who referred Jane Brolin to me.'

Maggie Eastwood filed for divorce from Wynberg on her return to California from London in August 1989. Part of her petition to the court was that Wynberg be ordered to stay away from her Pebble Beach home saying he was 'hotheaded and has been verbally abusive towards me in the past especially when he has been drinking'.

Wynberg was to remain in the spotlight by meeting up again with his old flame and drinking partner Elizabeth Taylor – in court. Wynberg, who in 1992 was married to nineteen-year-old Costa Rican Carla Golanz and living in Costa Rica, claimed he inspired Taylor's best-selling Passion perfume. 'I said in 1973: "Darling, your movie star career is over. You need something for your old age."' He argues that she did create her perfume pension but that he did not receive any cash or credit. In Los Angeles Superior Court in 1990 he sought $5 million in cash and an additional 30 per cent of the $70 million a year profits from sales of the fragrance. Eventually he agreed to settle for $4 million.

Maggie Eastwood's marriage to Wynberg is something Eastwood will not be drawn on and this, of course, is in deference to their children Kyle and Alison. But the family ties, the family matters, had all been troubling him for some time. He, as always, wanted control, especially over his children. But he was determined that he would never be involved in anything messy. His divorce from Maggie Eastwood had been controlled, contractual and quiet. He could never imagine himself getting into a public situation like Liz Taylor – appearing in court for two days before the proceedings were stopped by the out-of-court deal in the Passion case. But it was his need for control that was to result in his public mess. In a situation he had spent his career avoiding. The private man was going to be accused of a series of sins by his longtime lover Sondra Locke.

. . .

Eastwood, the world's richest star, was establishment towards the end of the eighties. The Man With No Name was joining the great names of the movies like Orson Welles, Frank Capra, Alfred Hitchcock and the Bergmans – Ingrid and Ingemar – and a host of others who had become the subjects of serious film study. The Clint Eastwood Cinema Collection was established at the Museum of Modern Art (MOMA) in New York and at the Wesleyan University Cinema Archives. MOMA was to preserve prints of his films from *Play Misty for Me* to *Bird*. Wesleyan University in Middletown, Connecticut, was to archive scripts and other papers, production material and memorabilia relating to Eastwood's career. Eastwood liked the preservation concept although he has always called himself a 'today or tomorrow man' rather than one who lived in the past.

Jeannie Basinger the curator of the Wesleyan Cinema Archives and Professor of Film Studies at the University says: 'We have been showing Clint Eastwood films in the classroom since 1971. We were honoured to place his papers in our archives along with other film artists – Clint Eastwood belongs in their company.' And so, he felt, did some of his wardrobe from the spaghetti Westerns: 'There's a poncho that's close to my heart – it sort of started me off – that's there.'

Elevated as a film artist in late 1988, Eastwood was also rolling along making *Pink Cadillac* with the statuesque Bernadette Peters as his co-star. It was *Any Which Way* type stuff except his co-star sported an eye-catching 36–24–36 rather than lots of fur. Eastwood was a bounty hunter who gets involved with Peters who is on the run in a 1959 pink convertible De Ville. Peters was initially concerned about Eastwood's reputation for not doing a lot of film takes – his more wham-bang-thank-you-ma'am school of film-making:

I was worried about that. But then I just fell into the swing of it, which is to capture the moment by what happens. You can't do that with every actor, but Clint is so right there, that he makes it easy, to work off each other. I learned a lot from him in doing the movie. It was a good lesson he taught me.

And you do work fast, which Clint has a theory about. It's so you don't hang around all day waiting for the set-ups. You don't get sluggish. You don't get distracted or lose interest. You don't forget where you are. It's a good way to work. It's so relaxed and that's so unusual. There's no pressure at all. I just said to myself: 'Oh, boy, this is great – enjoy it.'

Eastwood's work style is much admired especially in the cost-conscious Hollywood style of the nineties. Terry Semel is president of Warner Brothers, the studio which has distributed Eastwood's films since 1975:

People think of Clint Eastwood as a movie star and they know him as a director as well. But behind all that he is in effect the chairman of his Malpaso Company and he oversees every inch of every one of his films. During his tenure here he has been the most reliable and organized maker of films we've dealt with. Clint's a person who knows himself well. He's a very smart business man, always on or under budget in a day and age in which costs have escalated.

Warner Brothers would be pleased with him – he accounts for 18 per cent of their revenues from movies. That does not include the $1.5 million that go on the books every week from world-wide distribution of Eastwood movies on television, cable television and video – what's amusingly known as ancillary income. In what Semel calls an 'extremely unusual' arrangement, Eastwood works without a formal contract through Malpaso Productions. But informality is clearly one film for them, one for me. 'Very talented people have their ups and downs on certain movies but they will always prevail,' said Semel adding, 'The business we are in is about batting averages.'

There is no public record of what Eastwood's films have earned over the years but the last semi-official reckoning was in 1990 and the answer to the arithmetic was the staggering $1.85 billion gross. Considering his wealth, Eastwood has few indulgences or man toys. He has a French helicopter he bought in 1987 to commute between his home in Carmel and Los Angeles and there is what he calls 'a bunch of stuff'. From his teenaged days it was always women and cars and cars and women. In 1992 he owned several cars including a 1965 Plymouth police car, assorted trucks, a VW convertible, a 1932 Ford roadster and a 1986 Mercedes 500SL. He has also supported many charities anonymously, many of them to do with the environment, but long before green became fashionable.

It is also claimed that he and actor William Shatner, Captain Kirk of *Star Trek*, helped finance a private raid on Laos to free American prisoners of war. Retired green beret Lt Colonel James 'Bo' Gritz told the *Los Angeles Times* that he led mercenaries in the raid that was code-named 'Lazarus'. They had heard, he said, that about 100 Americans left behind after the Vietnam War were being held in a village 100 miles east of the Mekong River on the border between Thailand and Laos.

Gritz claimed the operation had US government support and his men were equipped with 'nuclear fire-plan boxes' with which they could communicate with mission members in Washington. Three days after going into Laos, the mercenaries came under mortar and assault rifle fire: one was killed and three badly wounded. Gritz who was decorated for services in Vietnam and Special Forces activities in Latin America had been involved in two other attempts to locate POWs. Eastwood would never confirm that he helped finance the abortive raid by putting up $20,000 for the film rights. Shatner said he gave $6500 as part of a payment for the rights to Gritz's life story.

'Clint has an extremely responsible way of working,' says Malpaso producer David Valdes who by 1992 had been part of the Eastwood team for nearly thirteen years. 'He spends each dime as if it were his own.' And given his wealth, he has every reason to believe it is.

Although low-key and easy-going, a man who does not flaunt his wealth and who plays down his Dirty Harry image, like all celebrities, Eastwood has always been aware of the dangers of extortion, kidnapping and crazed fans. Since 1983 he has had a permit from Monterey County officials to carry a concealed weapon, a .38-calibre pistol. In his application to Monterey Sheriff's department he wrote that he was the victim of 'various death threats against my life including that of kidnap in 1978'. FBI officials in San Francisco said they investigated the 1978 case but have never revealed the results. Eastwood has renewed his gun permit annually.

Stronger evidence to justify Eastwood's fears came in 1992 when he was involved in an incident with a real-life twist to *Play Misty for Me*. Brian Keith Nuen had been an Eastwood fan since he was eight years old. By 1992, at the age of thirty, he could be classified as an obsessed fan. He made a series of threatening calls to Eastwood at the Malpaso production offices on the Warner Brothers studio lot at Burbank, threatening Eastwood and the actor's family if he did not pay $5 million. The calls were made between 4 March and 29 March, 1992, and were recorded on voice mail. On tape a man identified as 'Brian' said God told him that Eastwood owed him money for three films and that if Eastwood did not pay by 11 April 1992, he would die within two weeks.

In one of the calls the message demanded a Jaguar, a pick-up truck, a gun rack, a rifle, a cowboy outfit and money for petrol as well as compensation 'for all the bills that you told me you'd reimburse me for when I came out to California for the first time via your guardian angel wavelength'. On a 4 March 1992 message, the caller said:

> *Hey, Clint, we have a compromise – just send me the $5 million cash . . . thank you for the responsibility for being my guardian angel in the first place and everything you get that went with it. Just send the cash by 11 April that's $5 million, US currency, and we'll work the rest out later – thanks a lot, goodbye.*

Nuen – Eastwood told the FBI he had never met him or heard of him – was arrested in Ellicott City, Baltimore. He told special agents that although he had made explicit death threats, he, himself, had no intention of killing Eastwood. He said he would not discuss his relationship with Eastwood without the actor present, said Agent Bill Hargreaves. Included in Hargreaves' official report is the following:

> *Nuen related that if the deadline was not met, Eastwood would be in a horrible moral and ethical position. Nuen stated that he did not expect Eastwood to live longer than two weeks after 11 April. Nuen related he would not harm Eastwood – he believed that God would handle the situation.*

In May 1989, Eastwood had other obsessions on his mind. On 28 May that year, he was to fly to Africa to make *White Hunter, Black Heart* a thinly disguised portrait of legendary film director John Huston's quest to shoot an elephant rather than get on with filming 1952's *African Queen* with Humphrey Bogart and Katharine Hepburn. And his private life after more than thirteen years with Sondra Locke had hit the fan.

.   .   .

From Los Angeles or San Francisco you fly over to Salt Lake City in Utah and then pick-up a twin-engine prop plane which takes you over the mountains to Sun Valley, Idaho. It is rugged Hemingway country and along the main street in the Sun Valley capital of Ketchum the walls of the bars and restaurants are covered with memorabilia of the macho-man author. This is a real man's Aspen. 'People here like to ski hard and play hard,' says actor Adam West who played Batman in the 1960's campy television series. West has lived on the outskirts of Ketchum for more than a decade:

> You don't see a lot of posing going on the slopes here. People come to ski and they're usually people who like a good party. Someone like Clint doesn't get bothered here. He just gets on with having a good time.

In 1988 Eastwood needed a good time. While he had filmed *The Dead Pool*, he had edited *Bird* – and taken it to Cannes – and he had committed to doing *Pink Cadillac*. He was running hard. And then the former mayor had authorities after him for being 'dirty'. That summer health inspectors found violations 'too numerous to list' at Eastwood's Hog Breath's Inn. Monterey County's environment health director Walter Wong said there was inadequate refrigeration, unsanitary conditions, improper food storage, structural problems that made it difficult to clean the kitchen and an 'extremely dirty kitchen'. Mr Wong reported: 'The dangerous part was that the refrigeration was not working. Food is supposed to be kept at 40 degrees – this was at 68 degrees.' Health inspectors closed the kitchen and Mr Wong said:

> If it gets to the point where we think food poisoning is possible or there are excessive violations, then we close it immediately. I really couldn't justify letting them remain open when there was a potential for people getting sick. I think they pretty much agreed with us.

The Hog's Breath bar stayed open. Work began on the kitchen and it opened again two weeks later. Eastwood was not happy with such a negative thing happening. It was just another hassle in what was turning out to be a trying year.

Yes, he did need a good time – and time to himself. His relationship with Sondra Locke was extremely rocky. They had become more and more estranged while he was Mayor of Carmel. He didn't encourage her to visit him in the town and he was enjoying the single life. 'He flirts around but he's very much a gentleman,' says Steve Strnadk who is the bartender at Bud's Pub Too. Playboy? Strnadk smiles: 'I've never seen him put the hard hustle on a woman.' But the town's favourite son also enjoyed the freedom of just hangin' out at Bud's where he and a group of male cronies are known as 'the barnacles'.

At fifty-eight, Eastwood was not so much set in his ways as cemented in them. In Sun Valley, he was friendly with Barbara Minty the former wife of screen idol Steve McQueen who died in 1980 from a heart attack during a cancer operation. Eastwood and the stunning former model who was thirty-three in 1988 were seen out at dinner and dancing at the Ketchum Country Club, a country-and-western bar/restaurant. And Sondra Locke believed there were other ladies.

Nevertheless, at Christmas that year, she and Eastwood did what they had been doing for the past seven years and flew to Sun Valley where they owned a holiday home – and where there was an almighty row which exploded over a series of concerns and frustrations on both sides. Eastwood wanted his son Kyle to live with him and Locke at his home in the rich Los Angeles suburb of Bel-Air but she wasn't sure. She was nagging him about his dates and remoteness. He never wanted to talk about their problems. And the more she complained, the more ticked off he became. He retaliated over a longtime sore point – her husband. Locke maintained her 1969 marriage to West Hollywood sculptor Gordon Anderson was never consummated. They were childhood friends in Shelbyville, Tennessee, and after their marriage moved to Los Angeles – Locke calls their relationship 'tantamount to brother and sister'.

In 1982, Eastwood had bought a house on Crescent Heights Boulevard in the Hollywood Hills for Gordon Anderson to use. The understanding was that this was a gift for Sondra Locke. But, in fact, strangely, both Sondra Locke and Gordon Anderson were named on a lease of the property with regular rent due to the landlord – Clint Eastwood. And the rent was paid from a joint Locke/Anderson account.

When Eastwood and Locke began living together in 1977 they moved into the house in the up-market Los Angeles suburb of Sherman Oaks where he had lived with Maggie Eastwood. Locke felt uncomfortable there living among the trappings of Eastwood's earlier life, among the family photographs and memorabilia. She talked to Eastwood about it and he told her that if she found a house she liked he would buy it for her. She found one – quickly. The two-storey stucco house with Spanish-tiled roof offered 5000 square feet of Bel-Air living space but was in need of renovation. Eastwood spent $1,125,000 for the property and Locke spent the next three years redecorating it. It sits behind high fences and electric gates.

The Sun Valley house also has a security system and the surprising thing was the Eastwood-Locke squabble didn't set it off. The screaming ended when Eastwood ordered her to return to Los Angeles. She did. And, after all the years they would only spend two more nights together. In January 1989, she and Eastwood talked about ending their relationship and some sort of settlement for her. Then, she consulted Los Angeles lawyer Norman Oberstein who assured her that something would be worked out amicably. No one, it appeared, wanted any fuss. And anyway, thought Locke, the relationship would soon be back on even keel again. As she and others have said many times – you never know everything that Clint Eastwood is thinking.

In the matter of Locke vs Eastwood the pack of cards that was left of their relationship began collapsing on the morning of 3 April 1989, when Locke took an early morning phone call at the Bel-Air house. It was Eastwood on the line. They needed to talk. He would be right over to the sprawling home they had shared on and off for more than nine years.

Eastwood did not hedge around what he wanted to say. He said Locke was sitting on his only real estate in Los Angeles and he wanted her to move out of the house. Dismayed, Locke told Eastwood she could not believe that's all he could say after their thirteen years together. Despite all the arguing and tension this was the moment she first really understood that their relationship was ending. Locke who had her forty-second birthday three weeks later saw her life vanishing before her. She was shaken. And she was tired. She was directing her second film, the thriller *Impulse*, at the time and had had only four hours sleep the night before. She begged Eastwood to stop any more talk about them breaking up until her film – starring Theresa Russell as a cop undercover as a hooker – was completed. He appeared to agree. He if anybody understood the pressures of film-making. They would talk again after she had finished *Impulse*.

The days rolled on, filming *Impulse* on location on the streets of Los Angeles. On 10 April Locke received a letter on the set of her film. It was addressed to Mrs Gordon Anderson. It was from Eastwood's lawyers and read in part:

> *Mr Eastwood has asked you to vacate the premises. You have refused to do so. This is to let you know that in view of your intransigence the locks on all the entrances of the house have been replaced . . . your possessions accordingly will be placed in storage.*

Sondra Locke fainted on the set of her film. A guard was placed at the Bel-Air property to ensure she did not enter it. She says that in 1992 she still didn't fully understand the emotional explosion but tried:

> *Maybe it was all the pressure of having so much power for so long, maybe it was the pressure of life goals, maybe a person reaches a*

certain age . . . He came to that point and I think, unfortunately, the sad part is that it couldn't be dealt with in a friendly, humane way.

It became, instead, a fierce battle. She was making her film, barred from her home and living with friends and with her husband Gordon Anderson at the Crescent Heights property in the Hollywood Hills. She had to borrow clothes from friends. She had no idea where her 1971 Mercedes was or the whereabouts of her adored parrot, Putty. Distraught, she went back to lawyer Norman Oberstein. He listened to her story and they decided to try and resolve matters by writing a 'strong' letter to Eastwood and his attorney Bruce Ramer. The four-page letter dated 24 April 1989, read in part:

Clint had obviously timed his 'blitzkreig' assault to maximize the emotional harm inflicted on Sondra. Clint also knew that Sondra was engaged in the most important professional work of her career and was preparing to shoot a difficult and key scene in the picture. If it gives you and Clint any personal pleasure or sadistic satisfaction, you did your work well – Sondra collapsed on the set and was left an emotional wreck. It is all she can do to hang on and complete her work – which everyone recognizes is the key to her future independence.

Why you and Clint are bent on a course which could cripple her ability to function and thus jeopardize her future independence escapes me. Why you and Clint desire to inflict on Sondra what you both knew would be intense personal pain is equally puzzling . . .

When Sondra consulted me in January, I concluded that Sondra's best course was to have patience and give you and Clint time to work out a settlement proposal . . . I was obviously mistaken in assuming that Clint would be reasonable, fair and responsible.

I even went so far as to incorrectly opine that Clint would not take the law into his own hands, harm Sondra, or seek to eject her from the house without benefit of court proceedings and some notice. I based that assessment of Clint on the good reputation he enjoyed among the people who knew him best, upon my own pleasant dealings with him, and upon my belief that a deep-pocket defendant with top-notch lawyers would not risk the exposure generated by lawless self-help. I won't make that mistake twice.

Oberstein went on to criticize Eastwood's behaviour as a 'well executed, calculated and cruel plan'. And then he was to open the way for headlines around the world with:

The insensitivity and cruelty which marked the manner in which Sondra was summarily ejected . . . without notice or warning is truly unparalleled in my experience. I promise you, however, our objective is neither to garner the last dollar nor obtain a settlement in light of Clint's substantial ability to pay; rather it is to meet Sondra's minimum expectations in light of a thirteen-year relationship.

Oberstein outlined his client's claim:

A one-time flat payment of $250,000.
Four years of financial support of $15,000 a month.
One year at $12,500 a month.
One year at $10,000 a month.
One year at $7500 a month.
Ownership of the Bel-Air house.
Ownership of the Crescent Heights house in the Hollywood Hills.

Attached to her claim was an outline of a palimony action she planned to file in Los Angeles Superior Court if her claims were not met. Under Californian law, unmarried couples have the right to sue for a 50/50 share of all assets acquired during the time they lived together. The precedent of 'palimony' was established by Hollywood divorce lawyer Marvin Mitchelson when he represented one-time actress Michelle Triola in 1975 in her landmark case against the late Oscar-winner actor Lee Marvin.

Sondra Locke's case was more complex. She was still married to Gordon Anderson so she would be a woman married to one man suing for palimony from another if Eastwood did not accept her terms. Eastwood got lawyer Bruce Ramer to inform 'Mrs Gordon Anderson' that her terms were not on. Angered by the tone of her lawyer's letter he was not willing to pay her off with $1.3 million and the two houses. And on 26 April 1989, he was slapped with a $70 million lawsuit. It didn't make his day.

EIGHT

It's a Jungle Out There

'Love – that's the key to any man. I think in the last years of his life that has been one of his lesser productions. He probably has to beat women away with a club.'

AUTHOR PETER VIERTEL ON EASTWOOD IN 1990

O n the third floor of Los Angeles Superior Court on Spring Street in the city's downtown there is a special section which is guarded at all times. The files are behind a wire cage and inside a court official warily watches over them. File C722032 tells the love/hate story of Clint Eastwood and Sondra Locke. Judge William Hogoboom who is retired from the Superior Court bench was brought in to referee the couple's estrangement. On 31 May 1989, he agreed to hold hearings behind closed doors at a secret location in West Los Angeles to stop any circus atmosphere following on from Locke's palimony lawsuit. This wasn't settling out of court – it was trying to settle in camera. And it was after the case had been set to be heard in public in the court of Judge Dan Senit Henry on the same date.

But Eastwood's lawyers had pressed for private hearings and whatever influences Eastwood had certainly worked. To a degree – for Locke's lawsuit leaked all over the world's front pages. If lawyer Oberstein's letter had been strong, then Locke's 22-page lawsuit was heavyweight vitriol. She contested:

> *From the start of our relationship Clint told me that he wanted us always to be together and that he would take care of me for ever. Clint repeatedly assured me that regardless of whether we were married, everything he had was ours together.*

In return, she undertook wifely duties, tending to the household, social activities and 'Eastwood's personal needs'. She asked for unspecified damages although with Eastwood's wealth estimated at around $140 million she would be able to claim at least half that amount. She also wanted the two houses in the Los Angeles area as well as an equal division of other property. And she wanted the court to order Eastwood to stay away from the Bel-Air estate 'because I know him to have a terrible temper . . . and he has frequently been abusive to me.'

Locke described the man she had loved for more than a dozen years as volatile and distant. She said he persuaded her to have two abortions which he himself arranged. And he talked her into having a sterilization operation known as a tubal ligation. 'At his specific request I underwent a tubal ligation,' she alleged in her lawsuit. She also claimed that by being locked out of the Bel-Air home she had 'suffered humiliation, mental anguish and severe emotional and physical distress and suffered mental and physical harm'.

After the lawsuit was filed an American newspaper quoted Locke alluding to Casanova Clint and saying: 'I'm going to make sure the court knows every woman Clint's spent the night with – I'm going to go all the way back to how he started living with me before he got a divorce from Maggie.'

It all made Eastwood shudder. Throughout his career he had been able to separate his public and private lives. But now? He was angry and he didn't want to give in to pressure – but did he want his life paraded through open court? Officially Eastwood made only one public comment: 'I am deeply disappointed and saddened that she's taken this kind of action. It will soon come to light that these accusations are unfounded and without merit, however, this matter will be dealt with in an appropriate legal arena.'

Eastwood was shaken by all the attention on his private life. Here was a man who objected to his home town being dubbed Scrooge City. And here he was being described as some evil-tempered fiend. He did everything he could to introduce some kind of damage control and got the co-operation of Judge Hogoboom to take the case into secret arbitration. The judge sealed all documents in the case and Eastwood's answers to his former lover's charges have never been made public. But in file C722032 he specifically rebuts Locke's charges about the abortions and sterilization – not that it happened but who made the decision.

In his secret legal papers he says: 'I adamantly deny and deeply resent the accusation that either one of those abortions or the tubal ligation were done at my demand, request or even suggestion. As to the abortions, I told Locke that whether to have children or terminate her pregnancies was a decision entirely hers. Particularly with regard to the tubal ligation I encouraged Locke to make her own decision *after* she had consulted with a physician about the appropriateness of and the necessity for that surgical procedure.' The 'Locke' must have hurt her. But was it better or worse than 'Mrs Gordon Anderson'? Later, Eastwood would call her in a conversation 'the person'.

Sondra Locke had made an Oscar-attention début in film with 1968's *The Heart is a Lonely Hunter* and it was a promising beginning but her identity rather got lost on celluloid after that. The ethereal-looking actress made six films with Eastwood but she was always part of the Eastwood ensemble and never really the co-star. She got the biggest part towards the end of their relationship in *Sudden Impact*. Eastwood was trying to give her more of a platform in the same way he would encourage her to go it alone by directing *Ratboy*. Locke enjoyed her role as Jennifer Spencer out to kill a team of rapists but nevertheless she felt, as she had throughout their relationship, that she walked in the tall man's shadow. She was never regarded in Hollywood as more than 'Eastwood's girlfriend'. She knew it and she accepted it. She could get people on the telephone because of her connection but that didn't change their perception of her.

After the palimony action she reflected on what had happened:

The total control men like him exert can be terrifying. Women get sucked into it because they want to please but it's dangerous for there is no compromise with absolute power. Clint had been both my lover and the father I was never really close to as a child. I was too dependent. Love, to me, meant absolute trust. I gave Clint my all, holding nothing back and demanding nothing. It's a feminine failing. I thought Clint and I would be together for ever then suddenly it was all over. I was devastated. I thought I'd been annihilated. I'd put so much of my life into this man's hands and suddenly it was gone. I felt as though I'd lost thirteen years of my life. I never really thought it would happen. When you find yourself in an unfurnished apartment with not one thing that represents what you'd thought you'd worked for you wake up one morning and, like Twilight Zone, *somebody says: 'Hey, too bad, you've gotta start over.' My objective was to be treated with some kind of respect. To be without my home, my books, my records, my fairy-tale collection – everything that defined me for thirteen years – is not fair.*

But during that thirteen years she had stayed married to Gordon Anderson – who was forty-four in 1992 – who remains a man of some mystery. He stays behind the gates of the Crescent Heights home in Hollywood and has never spoken about the bizarre set-up involving him, his wife and Eastwood.

Sondra Locke kept a wardrobe of clothes and make-up at the $650,000 house which she and Anderson found and which Eastwood bought. She would spend days at the house, cook dinner for her husband and then go back to her lover for the evening. Eastwood paid all the utility bills at the Crescent Heights house and felt he was 'taken for a ride.'

Judge Hogoboom held a series of private hearings on the palimony case. Everything was kept secret but he did give Locke 'interim relief' allowing payments to her while the negotiations were going on. And they went on and on. Finally, the judge ruled that there was no palimony case as Locke was married throughout her relationship with Eastwood. This was in the summer of 1989. But the ruling was in arbitration and not legally binding. Locke refused to accept the decision and pursued a full hearing in Los Angeles Superior Court. Eastwood left the negotiations to his lawyers and flew to Africa to confront altogether different beasts in *White Hunter, Black Heart*. Sondra Locke had also carried on working with *Impulse*. Her star, Theresa Russell, believes the movie helped Locke cope: 'I talked to her and said: "Maybe it's a good distancing thing." It seemed to work out because she is basically a strong person.' But Eastwood was also showing his strength and refusing to give in on the palimony action. There were lots of telephone calls between California and Zimbabwe.

.   .   .

Eastwood was getting fed-up with women and lawsuits in 1989. First, there was the palimony action. And then along came Stacy McLaughlin who worked for an animation company in Universal City, a ten-minute drive from Malpaso Productions at Burbank. McLaughlin had to drop off a video-tape at Eastwood's office. She did. She also parked in his spot. Now, parking spots at Hollywood Studios are like goldmines – when you get one you hang on to it. There was a story going back to the seventies which had an angry Eastwood taking a sledgehammer to a car parked in his spot. 'A myth,' says a Malpaso worker explaining: 'What happened is a gentleman who used to be Clint's producer took a hammer and went out and beat in the windshield of a car that was parked in Clint's space.'

Depending on how the mood takes him, Eastwood has two methods for those who invade his space parking-wise. If the keys are in the ignition he will quietly drive the vehicle to the furthest point on the back lot of the studio, park it and walk away without saying a word. If things are more hectic he has been known to nudge cars out of the way with his truck without damaging them. McLaughlin claimed she got the nudge, nudge. She said she left her car in Eastwood's spot while she went to visit another producer, Paul Maslansky, and in Maslansky's office she was told by a security guard to move her car. When she returned it had already been moved.

McLaughlin sued for $1000 for damage to her car and $100,000 in punitive damages. When the case was heard in Burbank Municipal Court, Judge Marion Gubler ruled in Eastwood's favour. And she ordered McLaughlin to pay the star's legal costs. In turn, Eastwood, who said he was only trying to park his quarter-ton weight pick-up truck in its rightful place, paid $960 to repair the headlight and bumper of McLaughlin's car.

Eastwood was becoming a little teed-off at the way things were going for him; suddenly, he didn't appear to be in control. In Africa, he was.

Writer Peter Viertel – he is seventy-six now and lives in Spain with his wife, the actress Deborah Kerr – went to Africa in 1951 to complete the script for *The African Queen* for director John Huston. He was hired after James Agee, who adapted the script from C.S. Forester's novel, died of a heart attack. Huston was a legend even then – the director of *The Maltese Falcon* and *The Treasure of the Sierra Madre* – and as formidable as his films. The image was the reality: he was a hard-drinking, self-indulgent and passionate man. The writer watched Huston descend close to madness, the victim of a crushing obsession.

Viertel wrote a novel based on his experience in which he fictionalized the names of himself, Huston and producer Sam Spiegel. He wrote about the director's wild desire to kill an elephant and he believes today that Huston only took on *The African Queen* because it provided an opportunity to hunt big game – he treated everyone who did not want to hunt as a traitor. The writer believed Huston was squandering his talents and putting production of *The African Queen* – despite everything it still became an Oscar-winning classic – in jeopardy: 'John was a gifted film-maker but he was also a supreme egotist. He would get distracted by some personal whim and he would have his way no matter what.'

White Hunter, Black Heart was written in 1953 as a sort of anti-hunting, open letter from Viertel to Huston. There had been great rows between the two men but Huston offered to sign a release for the book before he had even seen it and Viertel recalls: 'After he read the first draft he suggested a different ending which I used and he never mentioned the book to me again.'

Eastwood was intrigued by the idea of Huston taking the money to make a film and then going off seeking the big tusker while his stars Katharine Hepburn and Humphrey Bogart idly sat around. You can understand his questioning such action for it goes so much against his own instincts. He never met Huston, who died before *White Hunter, Black Heart* began filming. But in the film he plays him in the guise of director John Wilson in both voice and manner. It was a s-t-r-e-t-c-h, and although many critics applauded Eastwood-the-director, they believed he had cast the wrong actor in the lead role. But he explained: 'What's the point of doing it if you don't stretch yourself?'

Which was also the creed of the at times macho-blustering eccentric Huston who in moments Eastwood catches eerily well. 'There was a lot of tension over Huston's obsession with elephant hunting and even in his book he talks about going off on a three-week safari, leaving his crew just sitting around,' said Eastwood adding: 'He admits to being possessed though he claims he never shot an elephant and Peter Viertel backs that up. Of course, I am sort of anti-hunting. I don't put down what anyone wants to do but it seems to me that killing creatures for fun is not a progressive idea. It's probably one of the oldest things that mankind's done but by the same token there's a certain kind of obsolescence about it. And I guess I just like animals a lot.

'But I was kind of interested in Huston's obsessions because he always seemed to have one, but more so on this film. Though he managed to make really fine films, there was seemingly some distraction on all of them, whether it was racehorses on one or a woman on another. Most people envision a fine film-maker as someone who puts everything in the world into his picture, but in his case it didn't seem that necessary.

'There was an incident that was supposed to have happened during *The African Queen* which Katharine Hepburn talks about. She was doing this scene with Bogart in the back of the boat and Huston was up at the bow, fishing. And she said, "John, you're not watching me." And he replied, "I can hear you, darling. I can hear you." Maybe he'd seen the rehearsal and kind of knew what was going on; maybe just keeping that partial attention was what his great talent was – to never get too wrapped up, to know when something was right.

'Before going to Africa, I looked at most of the documentaries on him and listened to talks he'd made, public-service announcements, and American Sportsman shows. I sat next to Anjelica Huston [his daughter] at a party and talked to her. She wasn't that familiar with that era in his life, but she did say that Peter Viertel's book probably had a little more truth than poetry to it.

'I just looked at a lot of Huston's delivery and thought in terms like that. He had a certain patronizing quality and a certain paternal quality, and I just thought about that and let it happen. His enunciation was a little bit conscious of the way he . . . you know, when he's talking to you, he's commanding everyone to listen in. It's very difficult with that particular kind of character not to want to . . . I mean, I used to do an imitation of him, but I didn't want to do an impersonation. Huston himself would have probably been much more exacting. He would have highlighted the characteristics – I just sort of took on the feeling.

'I guess I could have played it completely differently, but I kinda liked the Huston character. Some of the philosophies he expounded . . . Huston in life could be an extremely personable person but at the same time he could be very cruel to his friends and neighbours, depending on the mood he was in.

'I think everybody has had something that they've been obsessed about in their lifetime. Maybe it's large, maybe it's small. In Huston's case it was large – everything he did in life was large. He was a sort of bigger-than-life character. It was interesting because the character was such a dichotomy. On the one hand, he tried to rough-house, and on the other hand he was a self-educated man, an incessant reader. When he was a kid he was misdiagnosed with a heart problem by his doctors, and it was thought he was going to die at twenty-five. Maybe he thought, 'What the hell? I'm going to live beyond my expectations.'

You wonder what Peter Viertel's expectations were nearly forty years after he first went into the jungle with John Huston. *Déjà vu?* With Eastwood it was the opposite, of course. There was control. Viertel observed:

> *On the set I found him aloof. There was the feeling that he was the boss without any shouting or megaphones or tantrums. He withholds. I think he's a very shy man down deep. I think he is a man propelled by a terrific ambition. You have to make money for these bastards [the studios] otherwise they don't give you any more. But he doesn't want to be the richest man in the cemetery. He's a man with something to say.*
>
> *Love – that's the key to any man. I think in the last years of his life that has been one of his lesser productions. He probably has to beat women away with a club. But I'm not talking about sex. I'm talking about human emotions.*

It was more physical than emotional when Eastwood took *White Hunter, Black Heart* to compete at the 1990 Cannes Film Festival. Sylvester Stallone and Arnold Schwarzenegger were also there and the trio turned the town into muscle beach. The threesome were mobbed at the 43rd festival and Eastwood hugely enjoyed himself. He also liked the topless blonde. Interestingly, she was Californian and not French. She made her points. During a break in St Tropez, the resort Bardot made famous, Eastwood and Bruce Willis and half a dozen other film-makers were having lunch when Michelle Gray jumped on their table and stripped off. She danced for ten minutes while Eastwood forgot about his discreetly oiled *salade Niçoise* and concentrated on some other light dressing. Why was he paying so much attention?

'People's excessive behaviour fascinates me and Michelle put on a great performance. If you've got it, you should flaunt it.'

Of course, he didn't want to flaunt his private life. The palimony case was still lost somewhere in the spaghetti of paperwork at Los Angeles Superior Court. Eastwood was a little more vocal about it as time dragged on and he admitted: 'I felt so disappointed – and the disappointment was with myself. How could I spend so many years with Sondra? How could I have been such a bad judge of character? Everywhere I went I couldn't get away from it – it made me so uncomfortable.'

Eastwood felt the palimony lawsuit showed a 'double standard'. He had helped her find work as an actress and also encouraged her to direct films. Of the lawsuit he said: 'It's not at all classy. At some point a person has to make up their minds whether they want to be a film director or an ex-girlfriend. I gather the people who advised her thought I would be brought to my knees by some public humiliation. Well, they didn't read me right. They misread me by thinking that making false statements would flush me into some giveaway programme.' Valiant words, but discretionary tactics would follow.

.   .   .

Women! Women! Eastwood was also having to deal with personalities even closer to home. And, seemingly, always closer to him: 'I have always treated my kids as adults,' says Clint Eastwood of Kyle and Alison. 'I have never talked down to them. I just let them be themselves, allow them to make their share of mistakes. If you train them well they won't make that many of them.' His children grew into their teenaged years as the offspring of divorced parents but Eastwood and Maggie Eastwood have always been united, like any parents, in wanting to do the very best for their children.

Maggie Eastwood says Alison – a Gemini like her father – takes after the actor: 'They are independent, sure of themselves. They are fast moving people and they think fast. Now, Kyle's a Taurus, a bull, and of a completely different nature, he's steadier.' Kyle, six foot two tall, a film student, is lean and wiry like his father and says of being brought up by a superstar:

I'm pretty much used to it. People do think that my father is the same as he appears in the movies which he isn't really. It's almost like there are two people – sometimes it shows through in movies the way he really is but most of the time it's pretty much an act. Most of my close friends know. He's pretty much an ordinary guy in real life.

As far back as I can remember I remember being on movie sets. I was born during the filming of Where Eagles Dare. *I think the first set I was on was* Paint Your Wagon.

He says he always understood the need for his father to work and says: 'Maybe it was kind of hard – but there was a lot of good about being his son.' He played his own age – fourteen – in 1982 when he starred with his father in *Honkytonk Man* and was happy with the experience:

The wonderful thing was I was just being myself. I can handle myself but I don't go around saying: 'I'm Clint Eastwood's son.' My dad's a good teacher and he helped me a lot. It was a time to be close to him and I loved that.

Alison Eastwood says:

I know my father has a lot of pressures but he never piles them on me or my brother. He always has time for us. He's so patient – he's not the man you see on the screen. He's gentle and caring.

Eastwood's daughter has model looks. She's a slinky size six on a five foot eight frame with long, blonde hair and blue-green eyes: 'I have my Dad's squint – all I need is a cowboy hat and a little stubble.'

But that was not how the tall and willowy girl graced the cover of *Town and Country* magazine in January 1990. Photographer Tom Hollyman says: 'She's not just a pretty girl – she's arresting.' After that magazine appeared another called her 'the prettiest moving picture Clint's ever made'. She has been involved in modelling and, of course, Hollywood is always looking for knock 'em dead blondes. She was just eleven years old in 1984 when she appeared with her father, who calls his children 'sawn-offs', in the sex-thriller *Tightrope*. And that led to a fan travelling half-way around the world to stalk her. In 1989 Mike Joynson, a drifter, who was then twenty, left his mother's home in New Zealand to try and meet Alison. He had been obsessed with her since the film in which she played cop Eastwood's daughter Amanda who is hand-cuffed and bound by a psycho killer.

Joynson found his way to Pebble Beach near Carmel where Alison was living with her mother Maggie Eastwood in their spectacular Pacific Ocean-view home on California's world-famous seventeen-mile scenic drive. The family went to court to get a restraining order against him and Alison told the Monterey County Court:

> *In early 1989, he jumped the security fences and entered my mother's home where I lived without knocking, demanding to see me and give me presents, saying he'd madly wanted to see me since seeing me in the movie* Tightrope. *He left before security officers arrived.*

And then, just as suddenly, he returned a year later. Alison told the court of the 1990 incidents:

> *He's come to the entrance gate to my mother's house three times insisting on seeing me and has repeatedly phoned and faxed messages on unlisted numbers. He spent hours at Robert Louis Stevenson School trying to see me and slipped past the Pebble Beach gate guards and apparently started to camp out.*

Joynson arrived in Carmel on 14 January that year and booked into a $60 a night room at the Coachmen's Inn. He stayed in room 102 and a motel worker said:

I remember him. He was strange. He wore a Walkman all the time – even when people were speaking to him. He always used to lose his glasses and every day he would come to the manager's office looking for them. He always had a backpack on like he was ready to go somewhere.

Officials at Robert Louis Stevenson School from which Alison has since graduated had to chase Joynson away from the gates. Meanwhile flowers and gifts arrived at the house and Joynson at the security gates. On 17 January Monterey County police and Pebble Beach security officers became involved when they found Joynson had pitched a tent in a wooded area near the entrance to Alison's house. All that was in the tent was a locked suitcase. Police discovered Joynson riding a bicycle near the Eastwood home and a spokesman said: 'He admitted his interest in her and that he had sent her flowers and gifts although they didn't know each other.'

Later that day Sergeant Bruce Palmer says he served a restraining order on Joynson preventing him going within 500 yards of Alison. But Joynson was determined. Even Eastwood doing his Dirty Harry routine could not dissuade him, although when he confronted Joynson in a bar and told him to 'stay away' from Pebble Beach Joynson readily agreed. But within twenty-four hours he was in jail having been arrested on a disorderly conduct charge. His bail was set at $2000 and when he could not meet it he was held for five days in Monterey County jail. Joynson pleaded guilty to the disorderly charge against him and then left the country. It was another major worry for Eastwood.

And then Alison – who during an interview in May 1990, had shocked her mother by announcing: 'I could see postponing school for a little while' – dropped out of Santa Barbara City

College without finishing one term. There were reports of her dating older men and she was a fan of the heavy metal band Johnny Monster and the Nightmares. Alison was constantly at the band's concerts. For Eastwood, it was all beginning to turn out like every father's nightmare.

Alison was using fake identification saying she was twenty years old – the legal age for drinking in California – to get into night clubs. In October 1990, she went to see Johnny Monster and the Nightmares play at a club in Hollywood. Says one of her friends:

Once she was in the club she got loaded on booze right away. Then the band played one of her favourite songs and she jumped onstage with the band and started dancing like a madwoman. She was shaking and jumping so furiously that her breasts came out of her top. Alison was so drunk she didn't notice until some guys started to whistle and applaud. Then she laughed and put them back in her top.

After the club Alison drove her friends to Westwood, the university area of Los Angeles, in the 1988 BMW given to her by her father. She took one corner at 50 mph and skidded across three lanes, according to the Beverly Hills police report. Officer J. Sabbe's report says a breath test revealed her blood/alcohol level was .17 which was well above the California legal limit of .08. She was held in jail overnight. On 7 October 1990, Maggie Eastwood bailed her daughter out of jail. On 20 December that year Alison was fined $846 and sentenced to three years probation for drunk driving. Her licence was restricted allowing her to drive only to and from work or school. Clint Eastwood 'fined' his daughter the BMW. Since then he has tried to establish a closer rapport with a daughter who like him is headstrong.

Unlike him, she has an impulsive streak. In 1991 she was at a party in Hollywood when she met a striking thirty-year-old man – Chad McQueen the son of screen legend Steve McQueen. They were then seen out on dates and the gossip machine went into overdrive. By early 1992 they were 'planning marriage' and then Eastwood was supposedly begging them to live together rather than marry . . . and then they had broken up . . . but all the people actually involved have continued to maintain a dignified silence about a marriage which if it did happen would certainly have been made in Hollywood Heaven.

There was also talk of Eastwood getting married – to Dani Janssen the blonde widow of his army days acting friend David Janssen. She arranged a surprise sixtieth birthday party for him in 1990, but the wary Eastwood found out and trimmed the celebration down to dinner with a few friends. Blonde, beautifully turned out and manicured, Dani Janssen is a Hollywood ex-wife who divorced her fourth husband, stunt man turned director and Burt Reynolds' best friend, Hal Needham, in 1987. In 1992 she was fiftysomething. She was sixteen when she married Frenchman Donalde Crayne, twenty when she wed singer Buddy Greco, thirtysomething when she lived with and then marred David Janssen who died suddenly in 1980 and in 1990 was free again after marrying and divorcing Needham. Would Eastwood be husband number five?

—

NINE

Casanova Clint

'Try something new, always be open to a new challenge.'

JACK GREEN, EASTWOOD'S VETERAN CINEMATOGRAPHER

Dani Janssen's thoughts about someone rather than something old, something new and something blue were rather premature. When Eastwood began filming *The Rookie* in 1990 there was another lady around on the set of the buddy-cop movie. Red-haired Frances Fisher – something of a Sondra Locke lookalike – has starred in two extremely popular American daytime soap operas, *Guiding Light* and *Edge of Night*. She appeared in Eastwood's *Pink Cadillac* in 1989 and would later, in a career breakthrough, play legendary Lucille Ball in a television movie about the late comic actress and her one-time husband Desi Arnez.

There had been stories that the Eastwood/Sondra Locke fierce disentanglement had been forced on by his interest in *Pink Cadillac* co-star Bernadette Peters, but in fact the one that didn't get away was Fisher who turned forty in 1992. It was no surprise that she chose to be on the set of *The Rookie*. Eastwood was directing himself as veteran detective Nick Pulovski who is a specialist in car-theft rings. Charlie Sheen was playing his young partner. Raúl Julia was the mafia-connected evil mastermind. And Brazilian actress Sonia Braga was Leisel, the cocaine-snorting, karate-chopping hit woman for the thieves.

Braga arrived on *The Rookie* with a very sexy reputation. She was personally chosen by Eastwood for the role. Previously she had been romantically linked to Robert Redford after they made *The Milagro Beanfield War* together. This was a different sort of film for her. Cops and robbers. Car chases. The Brazilian actress was delighted with the change of pace. And she got to sexually assault Eastwood while as Pulovski he is strapped to a chair with his hands tied behind his back. It is the film's most erotic scene and a break in the relentless crash and bang of the car chases and constant carnage.

She rolled around the floor of a suite in the Beverly Hilton Hotel when she talked about working with Eastwood and it was

Above: In *Rawhide*, the series which changed everything for Eastwood, when as Rowdy Yates he became a television star. For seven and a half years he coddled cattle in 254 episodes of the show, which began in 1959 and became a hit around the world. *(VIACOM)*

Left: As the Stranger in Sergio Leone's *A Fistful of Dollars*. Eastwood, who had had enough of his role as hunky Rowdy Yates, reluctantly accepted the lead in the movie with the prophetic title. All involved got lucky. *(MGM)*

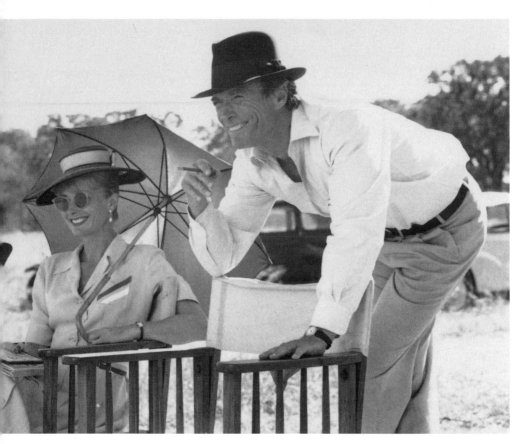

Above: In Africa on the set of
White Hunter, Black Heart, which
Eastwood directed in 1990 and in
which he also plays the part based
on film director John Huston, in
the guise of John Wilson.
(BFI STILLS, POSTERS AND DESIGNS)

Right: Film director, Don Siegel,
Eastwood's friend and mentor. It
was Siegel who co-signed
Eastwood's application to join the
Directors' Guild. For Eastwood's
début as a director with *Play
Misty for Me* in 1971, he used
Siegel's crew and persuaded him
to take a small part in the film.
(BFI STILLS, POSTERS AND DESIGNS)

Above: With Sondra Locke in *The Gauntlet*, in which Eastwood starred and directed. 'Many of my films have good roles for strong women. Sondra in *The Gauntlet* had more to say than I did'.
(WARNER BROS)

Left: As his directorial début, *Play Misty for Me* was a significant movie for Eastwood. In 1991 he revealed that it was based on a real story of sexual harassment. And it was Eastwood who was harassed.
(BFI STILLS, POSTERS AND DESIGNS)

Above: Kyle Eastwood on guitar.
(SCOPE)

Top: Kyle Eastwood on film with his father in *Honkytonk Man*. Sondra Locke was coach for young Eastwood when, aged fourteen, he was cast as his father's nephew.
(BFI STILLS, POSTERS AND DESIGNS)

Above left: With daughter Alison Eastwood, aged twelve, and Jennifer Beck, co-stars in *Tightrope*. In the detective drama, Alison plays Eastwood's daughter Amanda Block. *(REX FEATURES)*

Opposite top: Scrambling his way to the top. In 1968 Eastwood was paid $750,000 for his role in *Where Eagles Dare* and got the same billing as Richard Burton, who was by then an acting and marital legend. *(MGM)*

Opposite left: After working with him, the late Richard Burton said his co-star in *Where Eagles Dare* had 'dynamic lethargy'.
(TURNER PROGRAM SERVICES)

Above: The Dave Brubeck Quartet. Eastwood followed Brubeck, one of his favourite jazz musicians. In the army at Fort Ord, he met Lennie Niehaus, a former saxophonist with Stan Kenton, who later wrote the music for several of Eastwood's films and taught Forest Whitaker to play sax in *Bird*. *(REX FEATURES)*

Right: Forest Whitaker as Charlie 'Bird' Parker in *Bird*. 'There are two American art forms, the Western and jazz.' Eastwood's comment was appropriate to his art. With his Westerns under his belt, he fulfilled a longstanding ambition when he directed *Bird* for Warner Brothers. *(WARNER BROS)*

Top: Carmel-by-the-Sea, California, April 1986. A victorious Clint Eastwood accepts a different role—as mayor of Carmel—on winning the mayoral election. He earned $200 a month. On the longtime Eastwood movie policy of less talking, more action, he limited his speeches to three minutes.
(REX FEATURES)

Above: Out and about on mayoral business. When asked if he wanted to be known as Mr. Mayor, he replied: 'Nah, just Clint'.
(E. SANDERSON/SHOOTING STAR SCOPE)

Left: The Hog's Breath Inn at Carmel is co-owned by Eastwood. Here there are *Dirty Harry* hamburgers (cheese), *Magnum Force* omelettes (hot pepper) and Eastwood's favourite *Gauntlet* cheesecake (boysenberry).
(REX FEATURES)

Top: As the Stranger in *High Plains Drifter*. *(UNIVERSAL CITY)*

Right: Classic and classy Clint in *Coogan's Bluff*. *(UNIVERSAL CITY)*

Above: As Marine Gunnery Sergeant Tom Highway in *Heartbreak Ridge*. *(WARNER BROS)* easy to see why he was intrigued by the actress known as the Marilyn Monroe of South America. It has nothing whatsoever to do with her looks. Braga bombshells in an age when such ladies have largely been replaced by bimbos. There's a certain sexual explicitness that has little to do with titillation but more with bravado. In the land of coffee and dental-floss bikinis, she's been the nation's biggest star since Pele stopped scoring.

In *The Rookie* she is a kinky nymphomaniac and before she rapes Eastwood she plays around his chest with a razor blade then gets into torrid action. 'How did I seduce him? He was the director. He knew what he wanted.' Braga has her own goals. *Dona Flora and Her Two Husbands* and *Kiss of the Spider Woman* put her on the international, if art-cinema circuit. Robert Redford loved her and cast her in his mystical *The Milagro Beanfield War*. He had called her mystical and wonderful and all the other euphemisms which immediately make you believe he is sleeping with the leading lady and she offers similar words. But also the admonishment: 'I never lie. It is not true. There is nothing wrong with affairs, but I never had it.'

With Eastwood, the sex goddess from Brazil got into major mainstream movies. He offered her a chance to revel in her sexuality in *The Rookie*. Now she had even more reason to give hope to Brazilian womanhood. As Braga says:

They all wanted to be blonder and more blue eyed. They hadn't accepted their identity. They wanted to be Doris Day. Through my success they realized they could be five-feet-three with frizzy hair, brown eyes, wide hips and be beautiful. The audiences are my accomplices because I am the representative of a collective desire.

She has taken her clothes off for films and for magazines; but she is a serious person. Is this a serious person's performance? She talks in a sort of half-English by way of Garbo and Marlboro and bares all her uncapped teeth. (Brave stuff in Beverly Hills.) 'In

Brazil it is not unusual to do that if you are a singer or an actress. If you are asked to do it, why not? I am not ashamed of my body.'

She enjoyed *The Rookie* and the stunt people:

All the explosions and the pretending – it is my first action film and I've had a lot of fun doing it with all the kicking and running. It doesn't matter too much about the screenplay – you know what the plot is because it's always the same. But something happens with the action and the choreography, the big dance, the big ballet. People when they do action, they are very busy. Those are people who believe more in violence than in love. With the action everyone gets tense and the great lesson to me is that people are not too comfortable about love at these times. I want to do sex scenes as I do action.

Men? I can make them laugh. I tell them I love them and they laugh. They can't believe it. You tell them every time what they have to do to make you happy and they do the opposite because they don't want to be told. Which is good. If you do what they tell you then you will be together for ever and nobody wants that. All men are confused.

What about Eastwood who in *The Rookie* she makes love to in a scene involving bondage and sado-masochistic overtures?

I cannot sit on the set of a film thinking nobody is going to see it, so I am lucky that Clint chose me for the character. He is one of the best in action because of his background and that's why people will see the film.

The violence? When I was four years old I was watching Tom and Jerry and when I'm up there with a gun and I have to shoot somebody I'm playing out my earliest fantasy. I'm either Tom or Jerry. We don't read cartoons as violence. It's like being a kid in the circus seeing all these stunt people. They're making great cartoons – but making it spectacularly.

Yes, my feelings and my brain sometimes clash. We have a lot of discussions here with my brain because it's not everything I like that my brain agrees with. That's when you become repressive with yourself and you become prejudiced.

People are saying we shouldn't have sex in our life – you know what I mean? It's so primitive a thing, right? This is like nature. Normal. You should talk about love, you cannot talk about sex. Look at love stories. They kiss wrong. And you know because you've been kissing before . . . you know what a kiss is. A little one. A big one. It's good. It wouldn't hurt you. It's good. What's the problem?

Do you remember Last Tango in Paris? *Why was it this huge, huge event? Because it was so real. It was good, it was tense and it was open. It would be harder to make that film today. We continue walking backwards. We're becoming like to kiss is going to be difficult on screen.*

Frances Fisher's concerns were not about what was happening on screen. Sometimes she would wait for Eastwood into the early hours during night filming and they would take off for breakfast in his big red GMC (General Motors Corporation) truck. And, it seemed the Dani Janssen relationship was off despite cupid efforts by Frank Sinatra who was convinced Eastwood and Janssen should marry. 'They're perfect for each other,' he said.

Ladies? They were making life complicated. And his daughter Kimber by Roxanne Tunis was also putting on pressure from long distance. Things had become extremely strained between Eastwood and the girl born in 1964. By 1991 she had changed her name to Kimber Eastwood and had married for the second time, to Denver businessman Douglas McCartney. She claimed Eastwood wouldn't acknowledge her because she had talked about their father-daughter relationship:

I'm out of the family. I guess we never had the greatest relationship. He says I cut myself short by my actions. I'm upset because of my son Clinton but on the other hand His Highness can't bother me any more.

Eastwood, despite being given opportunities, does not comment on Kimber or Roxanne Tunis.

Despite all these romantic wanderings, Frances Fisher appeared to become a permanent part of Eastwood's life towards the end of 1990. They visited his home in Sun Valley, Idaho, and they were seen around Carmel and in Los Angeles. By early 1991 they went very public and went skiing together in Beaver Creek in Colorado's Rocky Mountains. 'I've known Clint for two years and we've been going out together for over a year. In love? Yes,' she said. 'He's a wonderful man and a special friend – it's nice to be together.'

As welcome as it must have been to resolve his palimony lawsuit with Sondra Locke. That was all concluded while he and Frances Fisher were on their Colorado skiing trip. Eastwood and his lawyers decided to settle with Locke five weeks before the case was scheduled to go to a jury trial in Los Angeles Superior Court in what would have been a very public showdown between the couple. It was a difficult decision for Eastwood. He had fought long and hard not to give in to Locke's demands which he felt reflected a 'double standard'. But discretion won out as he imagined the headlines around the world as his intimate life was stripped bare. It was a compromise he had to make. The amount of money involved has been quoted as anywhere between $6 million and $40 million. Neither side can legally reveal the exact amount but sources say it is much closer to the smaller figure. Locke also got the Bel-Air home and the Crescent Heights property in Hollywood where Gordon Anderson continued to live in 1992.

Locke's lawyer Norman Oberstein said the settlement followed a year of private negotiations: 'The matter has been settled and Miss Locke is very happy with the result,' he said. Eastwood won some concessions. Locke cannot ever sue him for more money. And he bought her silence. She can never write a book about him.

The actress had been going through a tragic time. On 12 September 1990, she had a lumpectomy at Cedars-Sinai Medical Centre in Los Angeles. A week later she was readmitted for a mastectomy and reconstruction of the right breast. She spent five days in a private room on the eighth floor of the hospital before leaving the medical centre on 25 September.

The breast cancer made her put her life in perspective. Until then she had thought the break-up with Eastwood was the most devastating thing that could have happened to her. Then, suddenly her life was in jeopardy. After the operation doctors could assure her that the cancer had not spread to her lymph system. The American Cancer society say that a woman whose cancer has not spread beyond the breast has a 90 per cent chance of survival. Locke decided on post-surgery counselling following her operation.

Eastwood was not around. Even given the then on-going palimony action this seems strange considering the years they had been together. Friends were quoted in American newspapers saying Eastwood had 'blocked off' Locke from his life. He himself has made no further public comment.

He has talked about love though: 'There are so many kinds of love. The love for one's children is hard to top. Sure, there's some battling that goes on. That's part of figuring out any relationship. Some people thrive on a violent kind of love – that's what works for them – and some want a serenity/tranquillity kind of love. As I've grown older, I've looked for more of the latter. It gets to be a kind of Zen thing, a plateau that you reach after you've been through everything else. The warrior ego gives way to something higher.

'The best kind of relationship is one where both people can express themselves freely and where there's mutual respect. I guess it's possible to love a woman and not respect her. But it wouldn't be anything that's gonna hang around for a while. Of course, everybody's in love in the sack. The question is: Are you in love five minutes afterward?

'I guess the line between love and infatuation is pretty slim. I always say if you can drive 200 miles with a gal and are still interested in talking with her, you know you're on the right track. But then again, you might drive ten miles and say, "God, I wish I left this girl home."' He's not left many at home.

.   .   .

With hindsight, it is interesting to see how those who were close to Eastwood over the years perceived him in their times with him. Eastwood is an icon and, like Bogart and Cagney and Gary Cooper and Cary Grant, people will be writing about him long after his final showdown. By then what people like Don Siegel and Sondra Locke have said will be archive material. Now, it is still very much of the immediate past or present.

Locke has said that she wishes Eastwood 'no harm in spite of everything'. In interviews, over the years they were lovers, she has said this:

Without question, Eastwood has it – and the 'it' in his case has a lot to do with good old-fashioned sexual magnetism. It's a certain magic that makes millions of people turn toward him like plants turning to light. When I see evidence of how popular Clint really is, it amazes me. Once when we were shooting a scene a huge crowd stood outside all day, waiting for him to appear at the door. And when he finally did, they sighed and oohed – they were enthralled. And the amazing thing is that Clint never thinks about his appeal. He never considers it.

He remains something of an enigma, even to his intimates. People can know him for years and never be sure of what he's thinking. He's one of the warmest people in the world, but there's a certain distance, a certain mystery to him. He's always unapproachable to some degree . . . . Clint is a rascal. The people I've enjoyed on the screen over the years have always had that element.

No matter how dramatic the moment in the film might be, there's a twinkle in the eye that says, 'I'm enjoying myself. I'm not taking myself too seriously so sit back and enjoy yourself, too.' All of them – Bogart, Cooper, Spencer Tracy – even at their most serious, always gave a subtle hint of slyness, of humour. Clint's a subtle actor, too. But because he seems so real, some people forget that he's acting. Yet to me, that's the ultimate in acting – when the character you play seems absolutely real.

Versatility is another Eastwood strong point. We were dubbing a couple of lines on *The Gauntlet* and at the same time preparing *The Enforcer* for television release. They threw a reel from each up on the screen, and the difference in Clint was incredible. That's how to best appreciate an actor – take small clips from his films and see how he brings a totally different feel to each role. Even his face changes. He can control his facial muscles the way Stradivari could control a violin. He can look primitive and violent one minute and then, when he breaks into a smile, he looks just like a little boy.

He's supersensitive, picks up on people's moods instantly – and he knows what's happening on every inch of the set. Never do anything you want Clint Eastwood to forget, because he remembers everything. He knows every single shot of every picture he's ever made.

When he's making a movie, he's incredibly objective – about himself, the other actors, the way the story is coming together. He's got a kind of third eye open all the time. He knows about lighting and sound and editing, and he can run all the equipment himself – so he doesn't shoot disconnected scenes, he shoots with the whole picture in mind. People tend to trust him because of that, so the atmosphere on the set is friendly but controlled. He doesn't need to shout like a dictator from the director's chair. People naturally respect him, so he just circulates, acting and planning shots and standing back and then acting again. He's a strong presence on the set.

I always saw something underneath those tough-guy roles that made him interesting – a hint of vulnerability, a certain boyishness and humour within the superman image. When we got to know each other, the boyishness became even more apparent. I've always been surprised that people don't pick up on it right away. That, and Clint's great sense of humour.

The forceful director Don Siegel was one of the old school of Hollywood. Much like the director Sam Peckinpah he had his own visions, and could make the camera create ballets out of the most violent situations by which he was able to stamp his work. He was Eastwood's film mentor and friend, and he died on 20 April 1991. Theirs started out as a head-butting relationship on *Coogan's Bluff* in 1968 but soon developed into one of mutual admiration. Siegel, a merry man with his moustache usually partially framing a smile, has said:

Coogan's Bluff was born out of chaos. I came on the picture after eight scripts had been written, and one director had quit. I found Clint very knowledgeable about making pictures, very good at knowing what to do with the camera. I also found that he's inclined to underestimate his range as an actor. I think he's a very underrated actor, partly because he is so successful.

We started out with cautious, mutual admiration. He started to come up with ideas for camera set-ups. I started to call these 'Clintus' shots and even if I decided not to use them they invariably gave me another idea, threw me into a 'Siegelini' shot. We've developed this and it's become fun making pictures with him.

We don't try to win points with each other. He doesn't try to impress on me that he is a big star and I don't try to impress on him that I'm a big director. If either one of us is really steadfast in an argument, whatever it is, the other has enough respect to realize there is something to it and give in.

Clint is a very strong individual, on and off the screen. He doesn't require, and I don't give him, too much attention. A good rule with Clint is that when you give him a direction, be sure you're right about it. If you don't think you're right, don't say it. Clint knows what he's doing when he acts and when he picks material. That's why he's the number-one box-office star in the world. His character is usually bigger than life. I think people don't really want to see pictures about mundane things and ordinary people. Clint's character is far from mundane or ordinary. He is a tarnished super-hero, actually an anti-hero. You can poke at a character like that. He makes mistakes, does things in questionable taste, is vulnerable. He's not a white knight rescuing the girl: he seduces her.

I particularly like the scene in *Two Mules for Sister Sara* in which Shirley MacLaine takes the arrow out of Clint's shoulder. It was done under difficult circumstances. The area was filled with ants. We used insecticides but they didn't do any good. Even without the ants it would have been a difficult sequence, particularly for Clint who is supposed to get more and more drunk as the scene proceeds. At the same time he had to show that a closer relationship was growing between them. It's my favourite scene in the picture and I felt they were both very good.

The Beguiled [1971] is my favourite film. I don't say it is necessarily my best film, but it's my favourite. This is a story about a huge, powerful, beautiful man, crippled in war, who's befriended and helped into a school, a sanctuary full of innocent, virginal girls – run by a headmistress whose virginity is caused by her frigidity. Behind the façade of innocent faces, when the chips are down, lurks just as much evil as in a group of hoodlums. Johnny McB is a beguiler. A man who thinks quickly on his feet. A con man. He sizes up every one of them . . . What happens is that Johnny McB unknowingly becomes a trapped man – helpless – by a bunch of sparrows.

There's a careful unity about the film, starting with the first frame. We begin with black and white and end with black and white, we start with Clint and the mushrooms and end with them; we start with Clint practically dead. And end with him dead. The film is rounded, intentionally turned in on itself.

The most important thing separating this from an ordinary picture, however, is not the rounding of the story, but the attitude of the females. For example, his murder, instead of filling the women with remorse, is followed by business as usual. Children are very cruel, and death doesn't have tremendous meaning. It doesn't happen to them. I tried to play that scene as if the women and girls were incapable of being touched . . . Women are capable of deceit, larceny, murder, anything . . . Any young girl who looks perfectly harmless is capable of murder.

Case in point: *Play Misty for Me* [1971], the first movie Clint directed [Siegel co-signed Eastwood's application to join the Directors' Guild]. He used my crew and persuaded me to take a small part in the film as the bartender. I wanted to be involved but I don't like being an actor. Clint tried to make me feel at ease but I felt so uncomfortable in front of my own crew. It was the first sequence he had ever directed in his life and it was the very first time I'd ever acted in a speaking role in a picture. I was extremely nervous and the only reason it apparently came off was because Clint was very kind to me and directed me very intelligently, so I calmed down and gave him what he wanted.

Later that year, Clint asked me to direct *Dirty Harry* [1971]. I saw Harry as a bigot . . . a bitter man. He doesn't like people. He has no use for anyone who breaks the law, and he doesn't like the way the law is administered. The killer was a personification of evil. I like my villains not to be stupid. Gosh, I want my villains to be brilliant, and that makes my hero that much more brilliant. I loathe those anti-Nazi pictures where the Nazis are a bunch of dopes. I mean, what are you defeating? For *Dirty Harry* we actually

162

printed only 60,000 feet of film. Of that we used about 10,000 feet in the finished picture. Now that is very little film for a Hollywood movie. Clint's famous for the way he hates waste.

In *Escape from Alcatraz* [1979] there were no stuntmen or doubles. Everybody did their own stunts – and their own fights. If there was any such position as stunt co-ordinator on this film, it goes to Clint himself. Shooting in the cells was interesting. Each cell is 5ft by 8ft. That's not much room to begin with and even less when you're shooting a 6ft 4in actor. But, thanks to Clint's co-operation, it worked. Clint's very strong and he can contort himself into any position you want him to assume. He would crawl in and out of the cell, climb up through the hatch into the ceiling, climb down the roof to the roof below. And if he had missed by a step he would have been killed.

From his early days as a film-maker, Clint Eastwood has surrounded himself with 'the Team', a unit which in more than two decades of movie-making he has strived to keep together. And the loyalty has been mutual. You just need to listen to the people he has worked with. A Clint Eastwood film is always an event. Joe Cavalier, who worked on five Eastwood films as assistant director and second unit director, singled out *Coogan's Bluff* (1968).

> *We had to find 600 or 700 people for the disco scene. We used 150 extras from the Screen Extras' Guild but the rest of them were all people I'd picked up from the streets, real flower children. Actually they worked better than the extras, because they would do anything you might tell them to do, and the other ones wouldn't. We couldn't let them go out to lunch – we figured they wouldn't come back. So we had to feed them on the set. There was one flower child . . . she wanted to go home at about four-thirty to feed her baby. I said, 'Well, we're on our last shot now, can you wait?' And she said, 'No, look at me.' And*

she opened up her robe and squirted milk. It went about four feet – she hit me right in the face with it.

It was hot water rather than milk that Cavalier thought he and Eastwood were getting in to with *Coogan's Bluff*. It contained one of Eastwood's earliest *risqué* scenes and Cavalier explained:

In the disco sequence Coogan comes across this high-wire girl who's partially nude. We had a discussion, Don Siegel and I, as to whether we should edit it out because of the censorship at the time. I thought it was the story's point, that she leads Coogan further on, and we should take a chance to leave it in, although in those days it was quite alarming. And, as it turned out, we asked the man in charge of censorship, and he felt it was important, too, story-wise; so we won that point with the censorship office. All I had to do as a trade-off was trim down the sequence where the nude woman is being decorated, later on, and the sequence where they are smoking marijuana.

The perfectionist trio of Eastwood, Siegel and Cavalier teamed up again in 1970 for *The Beguiled*. Realism is all important to them and Cavalier found the perfect solution to the sound Eastwood's character, the limping McBurney, would make when he walked. He brought in a one-legged extra.

All members of the team are involved in the decision-making and Carl Pingitore who was film editor said:

I've never worked on a film with such values. And Clint was very involved; once the first cut was finished, there was a real close collaboration between Eastwood, Siegel and myself. They're just two of the most brilliant men in the business and we were all working toward the same goal. We thought alike. There were times we were seeing a sequence and Clint would go, 'Huh?' and they didn't have to say what was wrong – just knew it. The Beguiled, Play Misty for Me and Dirty Harry were the most harmonious films I ever worked on.

Misty was Clint's first directorial endeavour and, I must tell you, he did a brilliant job. He was such a professional and had such instinct – it all tallied. Siegel has a small part in the film – he was a bartender – and he had such stage fright, but there was such affection and respect between the two men that Don insisted on being involved, and this gave him the opportunity. So he just did what Clint said, and Clint was marvellous.

Most people on Eastwood films do as the tall man says but he does let his crew enjoy freedom if things are going to plan. Bruce 'Spanky' Surtees, the director of photography on *The Outlaw Josey Wales*, says of them:

Clint's easy to work with because he lets his people alone. Whatever I wanted to do, I did. I've met a lot of directors and some of them think they know about photography and they hamper you more than help you. But if you get a good director who knows about staging and things like that, then it all fits together.

That admiration is echoed by production designer Ted Haworth, who worked on *The Beguiled*: 'It was a great satisfaction to work with Clint Eastwood, a man who has done it the hard way up, by his own bootstraps – a fine, creative, dedicated, unique man.'

Costume supervisor Glenn Wright is a long-time Eastwood employee. He chooses his words as carefully as he chooses his clothes:

Cost is something you have to be concerned with, of course, so you try not to spend money needlessly. But with Clint it really isn't a problem – he just wants you to spend your money wisely. He has no objections to your doing it, as long as you make sure you've got your dollar's worth, and it works for the film as a whole. Clint wears clothes so well it's easy to make him look nice – it doesn't have to be expensive. The toughest thing is to make him look bad.

Eastwood's penchant for keeping the team together led to Wright following in Siegel's footprints as a nervous 'star' in *Escape from*

Alcatraz (1979). It was another Eastwood-Siegel in-joke. Wright had to stand in the shower and hand out towels, using the same lines that he said in real life when he allocated clothes from the wardrobe. 'I didn't want to embarrass them or myself so I did my best,' says Wright. 'Then Don insisted I apply for membership of the Screen Actors' Guild and now I do a little acting as well. It's fun, but it's not easy. It's a challenge and it's hard work.'

Fun. Hard work. Perfection. These are the sort of words that you hear from the team. Steve Doroff, who has composed the music for a number of Malpaso films, says:

They were all a lot of fun. Particularly Every Which Way But Loose *[1978]. It was a ground-breaking film for Clint – it was really different. And it was at a time when country music was very popular. We had a very, very big hit record with it and it was the first movie that I'd ever done so I look back on it as being my favourite. It was real unusual, too. I remember looking at a rough cut of it before we started even coming up with the music and to be honest I didn't know what to make of it. I just sat there and laughed and enjoyed it.*

Something that made an everlasting impression on me was that as we were watching it, Clint would say: 'This is going to bring the house down,' or 'This is going to be great,' and even though I might have doubted it at the time, when the picture was finished and released, he was right. Clint really knew his audience and knew what would work.

There was another in-joke – a fun scene mimicking the Man With No Name. 'That was Clint, says Doroff. 'He just threw it out as an idea – "Why don't we do a Spaghetti Western kind of take-off?" and so we did it. It's a cute gag.'

Eastwood who seeks one talent rather than big names gave David Worth his big Hollywood break as director of photography on *Bronco Billy* (1980) – it was his first Hollywood break and the first time he had worked with Eastwood.

The crew was made up of people who had worked with Clint before. He works with basically the same crew year after year – Glenn Wright, who does wardrobe, goes all the way back to the Rawhide *days. A lot of his people – his property people, his special effects people, his costume people – go on and on and on with Clint.*

I worked with Clint exactly one year from the time I started to the time I finished – I did Bronco Billy *and* Any Which Way You Can *back to back, with just a couple of weeks break in between. I considered it to be my PhD in film-making. He was a real pro; very well prepared, someone who hires talented people and trusts them to do their job. During the year I worked with him I never heard him raise his voice once. He's a guy who's in charge, knows what he wants and knows how to get it.*

Seventy-five per cent of the time he prints on rehearsal or the first take. Of course, that gives a certain pace and confidence to the crew. On Bronco Billy *we actually finished two and a half weeks under schedule! I think that stands as a record to this day. It was valuable for me to realize that this was a man who has made hundreds of millions of dollars for the studios over the years; if he wanted to indulge himself, he could do it. No one would even bat an eye. But he was just the opposite. He absolutely detested the thought of wasting a penny that wasn't going on screen. This is the way I grew up working . . . and I found that all of the things I was doing out of necessity were being done by Clint Eastwood out of efficiency.*

It was very, very interesting. I'm in love with Bronco Billy. *I think it's a very endearing film, and, to this day, I believe it's one of Clint's favourite films. This is where I discovered what a generous actor Mr Eastwood is to his fellow performers. He went ahead and shot the master for the scene and then over his shoulder to the other actor, and then the medium shot, and then the close-up on the other actor before he ever turned the camera around on himself. His close-up was the last thing we ever did in the scene. He's not only an extremely well prepared director but also very generous to the other performers, saving his own shots for last when he's actually the best on the rehearsal or the first take.*

Eastwood covers all the corners, all aspects of the film-making process and Jack Garsha, a colour timer who has worked repeatedly with Eastwood, says:

Eastwood will use his editor, his cameraman, even his extras, over and over. You find out what he likes, and that's all there is to it. There's no sense in going through the same thing with a new timer for every picture. I mean, his people know what he wants and he knows they know what he wants, and you do your job, and he keeps out. You don't do your job – you're out.

Eastwood veteran, Jack Green, endorses all this:

You get what I call a 'finger-wave' rehearsal, which is: Clint tells you what the scene will look like; he'll give the actors instructions as to where they should be; he'll talk to me about the camera angles. With the actors unrehearsed, with the lighting and camera moves only worked out on stand-ins, he'll bring the actors in and 'roll on rehearsal'. Seven out of ten times, it'll be printed and we'll move on.

Film is like contemporary art. When you lose track of trying to find a new way to do something, when you become complacent, you become boring. I always want to have the Eastwood option, which is, 'Try something new, always be open to a new challenge'.

That other longtime Eastwood collaborator, Lennie Niehaus says:

I've done quite a few movies for Clint. I know how he works; the great thing about him is that he recognizes that each person he hires has his own creative ability and he doesn't want to thwart that. I see him do it with actors, too; he might give a few

168

suggestions but it's almost like, 'Let's see what you can do with it.' He makes everybody at ease.

Bird title star Forest Whitaker agrees: 'He's very cool, calm and very relaxed.' Whitaker's co-star actress Diane Venora felt the same:

I feel he trusts his people, from the top to the bottom. He knows who he hires, he likes what they are, and he trusts that they will work according to what he liked in them. He wants an uninhibited response so his feeling of not rehearsing is to create that off-balance for an actor. He exudes: 'I enjoy making films, I'll make them my whole life, it's a great place to be, I'm so grateful to have this as work.'

And that kind of generosity and love bleeds into everthing so nobody gets that uptight. There's never a moment of doubt who is in control of the set. He is truly that kind of director where there's never a hazy or grey area and that's a powerful thing because if you have a strong head, the rest of the body looks great. He is a Gentle-man.

Even the usually critical Norman Mailer, though not part of his team, is a major fan of Eastwood. He cites the moment in *Play Misty for Me* when Eastwood's character realizes that the girl he's casually dating is a dangerous psychotic: 'As the camera moves in, his stare is as still as the eyes of a trapped animal. Yet his expression is luminous with horror. He is one actor who can put his soul into his eyes.'

—

TEN

Self-Perception

'I like simple things, yet I'm obviously more complex than I appear on the surface.'

EASTWOOD ON EASTWOOD

Eastwood has always had the reputation of not being a talker but that is a misconception – a movie myth. He has only been reluctant to talk at any length about his private life. Nevertheless, he has always been willing to talk about himself and his work, and his views on that and on his public and politics are insightful to his personality. The world has changed dramatically since the late sixties when he became an international superstar but a decade earlier he was already a television name world-wide. Clint Eastwood has been an influence for more than three decades but although he talks with assurance, he makes his points quietly. Listen to him discuss his world during interviews over the past eighteen years and remember he's a man's man as well as a ladies' man.

'**I**'m at an age now where a lot of people have grown up with my films and gone through a lot of stages of their life with me. It means more sometimes when you look back.

'I don't wear make-up. I think it looks bad on men and sometimes on women and I don't wear it. If I look up on the screen one day and say, "OK, this is silly for the guy to be playing this kind of role," I'll step back and direct some films.'

Nevertheless, Eastwood maintains a rigid diet and exercise routine, although he insists: 'I'm not really a fitness fanatic. I just want to feel good. Some people think that when you're older you're supposed to sit down and watch TV reruns and squeeze beer cans. That isn't for me. I don't know if people want to meet me exactly. I get the feeling sometimes that people would rather have me pull out a .44 Magnum and say, "Do you feel lucky, punk?" They'd much rather meet the character than me.

'I've probably had as many profitable films as any actor around and maybe more. I just have to satisfy myself. Hopefully, I've made enough money for financiers in the business that I can afford myself a change of pace now and then. If you do a few small films you love and they're not commercial, they're sometimes better for you than doing a massive commercial thing that people take lightly. People may think more of you as an actor.

'Though I like Westerns and I like cop dramas, I'd hate to turn around twenty years from now and say: "Well, I did 900 cop dramas and 800 Westerns, and that was it." The truth is, I've done a lot of things. I just like certain movies. My performances vary a lot, a lot more than people think they do. Because I'm not an extroverted, extremely mobile type, I play things in reserve a lot of times, so people think my performances are similar. But if you place them side by side, you'll find they're quite a bit different. *The Outlaw Josey Wales* was really nice work – as good as I can do. *Dirty Harry* I thought was good, for a certain style that worked for me. It might have been harder for somebody else.

'Some actors try to show as much as they can. When you start in drama class, that's what you learn, to express as much as you can, express so much you tell the story without the dialogue. In your face. So, when you tell the story with the dialogue, it's a very expressive kind of thing. But if you look back through history, the people who have been the strongest in film were people who could express a lot by holding certain things in reserve, holding a certain amount in reserve so that the audience is curious to find what the reserve it. If you're reserved, the audience is constantly reaching forward to the character on the screen. If they sit back, they say, "OK, that was great, give 'em Four Stars for the news or something." But they're not interested in going back.

'I know I watch myself. I edit film of myself and I always have to look at him. Such as cut to him over there. I always think of "him" as another person on film. But in real life I'm not complicated. Yet, I am complicated, I suppose. I like simple things, yet I'm obviously more complex than I appear on the surface.

'Learning and refining and growing, that is what is fun about maturing in life. The downside is maturing, and the upside is maturing. Your tastes get broader and you appreciate things a lot more. You look back on things you overlooked as a youth and say: "My God, how could I have been that stupid?"

'They didn't have any schools in film when I started out, but they are quite popular now. I learned through hanging about. I have limitations, same as everybody. More than a lot of people. Certain things I do OK. Life is like a multiple-choice test. You can talk yourself out of the right answer most of the time if you think too hard and long about it. Most people have the ability to rely on their natural instincts, but too often they ignore them.

'I suppose I've regrets about a lot of things, but I don't think about those things. I look forward to what's going on now and tomorrow. If everybody dwelt in the past, you'd see them with tears in their eyes. Everyone's made certain mistakes they would have corrected if it had been possible, but it isn't possible so you just go on.

'As an actor I'm a little hard to understand, if you try analysing it. The public seems to understand me on an instinctive basis. Sometimes when people can't break something down, they get bugged by it. But I guess I'm kind of an oddity.'

An oddity? Well certainly one who has made a fortune. But as we have seen, he is not one to flaunt it.

'Sure, money is nice. I wouldn't want to be broke, but it doesn't mean much to me really. I don't have a lot of needs; I spend a little; invest a little. I just try to take care of my family and the people close to me. I get periods of being obsessed by work but when I play I just l-a-y back. I go through periods of just not wanting to do anything, maybe just sitting at home watching whatever's on TV. An actor's lament, of course, is you're always wondering where your next job's coming from and the plain truth of the matter is that the majority of the Screen Actors' Guild have a rough time making a living, just staying in that profession only. It's a tough profession. You have to really want it. If you're in it just for

the dough, then you'll get a rude awakening. And if you're lucky –
I use that word a lot – you can made a fine good living in the
profession. I never begged for respectability. I never said, "Come,
let me show you, come like me."

'I guess I can lie like anybody else, but I don't like it. I'd hate
to exist constantly, day-in, day-out, having to come up with
something. Having to come up with something whether it's the
truth, a variation of the truth or whether it's an outright lie or
variations on a lie. I don't really know myself. I don't think too
much of myself.

'I remember going on interviews – cattle-call type – with ten,
fifteen, maybe twenty guys all your size and colouring. Every
interview you go you see the same people. I was never very good at the
presentation at the office for some reason. I always got somehow dim-
witted. I met a lot of people that I suppose knew a lot, and I met a lot
of people that didn't know a lot, so I'm always very careful when I
interview actors not to put them through any undue stress. I don't
like to read actors because I can't stand to do that. I'll look at film
often while doing research before I'll ever meet them so that way I
never get their hopes up if I'm considering somebody else. It's more
work, but it's just a matter of sensitivity. Once you've been sort of
mentally kicked around you kind of become aware of that. There's an
awful lot of other people that are really good that are overlooked. I like
to try to reach out and grab them if I can.'

Eastwood's image is much more macho than mediator but he
has always thought of himself as a day-dreamer, from his school-
days making up stories and characters.

'I've always kind of meditated. I was a day-dreamer as a kid. I
just like being by myself and meditating. I think a certain kind of
meditation is good for anybody for some sort of peace of mind.
Some people find it looking at the ocean, some people find it in
religion. It depends on the individual. I don't believe in the old
adage that men shouldn't cry. If a person feels like crying it's

probably the greatest cartharsis in the world. I don't get as emotional as the next person, everybody reacts differently.'

But he's practical about what he describes as only 'the job'.

'I just figured I'd do the job. I remember when I was first starting out everyone used to sit around and argue about whether we wanted to be great actors or movie stars. Of course, everyone would say: "Well, I'd rather be a great actor" because that's the idealistic and noble thing to say. But then if you start analysing it, the movie star gets offered all the great roles. And it's nice to be in a position of power where you can generate the kind of roles you like to play.

'Everyone here wants to get side tracked – get in a series, make a lot of money. Of course, British actors like to make a lot of money too, but they take their work seriously. And generally speaking, American actors don't have the versatility. They do one thing well and that's it. I suppose I have to put myself in that category. Certain things I do are OK, I guess, but I'm not the kind of actor who'll play a 25-year-old bank clerk one day and a 90-year-old derelict the next.

'I was never a discovery of the press. I never had a publicity build-up or any amazing covers. I had to have the success first. I don't try to be a parody of myself. After I had acted for a few years and was thrown out of Universal and voted least likely to succeed as a contract player, I did an awful Western. It was so bad they didn't even show it to the cast and crew, they just put it out. When I finally saw it, I just slid lower and lower in the seat. I thought: "I've got to get out of this business, I've just got to get out." My wife at the time encouraged me, and I finally mustered up the sand and said, "I'm going to win this game." But I don't mind being pessimistic at times.

'Wherever I came from, I always came out of left field. I wasn't predicted to do anything. So it was easy to say that this guy was going nowhere. And then when he does try to do something, maybe that disappoints the soothsayers who've decided his type isn't supposed to do anything at all.

'I never second-guess audiences because many times they're just so much further ahead of you. And then sometimes, they miss what you think you've been explaining so simply. So, you can't second guess. All you do is build on your own instinctive reactions. That tells you what to do. You do it the best way you know how, and hope, of course, that somebody likes it.

'I can't be analytical about it, it's an animalistic kind of thing. Acting isn't a very intellectual art really, in fact it's not intellectual at all. People like to intellectualize about it and others like to make out it's a very misty thing but the basis for acting is very childlike, that's why children are brilliant actors – they can fantasize about anything. We just stack on the inhibitions as we grow up.

'There must be plenty of people a lot prettier than I am. I suppose somehow it is the combination of the way I sound, the way I think and somewhere in there I've managed to represent to people something that they like. They like an element of escapism and I evidently have been able to transmit some of the escapist thing. Men can probably identify more with me than the prettier actor. They might say: "I'd like to be able to do what this character is doing." And the female audiences – well maybe they'd say: "If I were involved in that story, I'd like to have this man on my side."

'Everybody has to play characters that suit them. Somebody else might try the same characters and it might not work. There are a lot of marvellous actors in the world with better training and schooling than me but if they'd played *Dirty Harry* it wouldn't suit them. Olivier would have looked ridiculous with a poncho and pistol.

'Everybody likes to draw a picture of you walking into a supermarket and a director coming up and saying: "Hey, you're the lead in my next movie," but that's a dream. Anyway, if that had happened I wouldn't have been prepared. It would have been a disaster.

'To some people I represent a dying individuality within our system. I feel there is a crying out for individuality. I feel that because of the intellect, the human race, we've bogged ourselves down in such bureaucratic nonsense, that it seems like we have made life much more complicated than it should be.'

He's been called complex. And complicated. Has he failings? Things he doesn't like about himself?

'I guess I am vain. I never thought about it. I don't look in the mirror and ask, "Who is the fairest of them all?" If you do that a voice comes out and says: "Snow White, baby, and don't you forget it!" I have never come to the point where I wish I was back a few years. I have always felt every year is always better than the last.

'I hate to be mauled. I don't like large crowds of people. I like people but I'm not that comfortable with them. I've been on film sets where after lunch, girls came up and asked for my dirty plate or empty beer bottle. It has a lot of downsides. You don't have a certain amount of privacy in your life and I am kind of a private person. Once in a while it has an upside. It can get a table down front or something.

'People like different things. Stardom enables you to get a front-row seat but it also means you are stared at, that you are constantly interrupted by people recognizing you, you're always the observed rather than the observer. But then people have spent their time viewing you, so you've had some effect on them through your entertainment, probably brought something into their life. You must consider that and accept it.

'I tell people if you really want to do it, you must be willing to study it and stick with it through all opposition and having to deal with some of the most no-talent people in the world passing judgement on you. They're going to pick the worst aspects of you or of anybody else they cast. If you can take all that and keep grinding until some part comes along that fits you and your feelings, then sometimes the odds will come up for you. But you have to have that kind of perseverance.'

Of course, he has often played that sort of role, the man against the odds and talking about his movies he warms to the subject.

'A lot of my characters are sort of the lone guy struggling against some element in society. I never felt any moral problems with these pictures. I felt they're fantasy.

'I don't think my movies are that stimulating. People in the audience just sit there and say: "I admire the independence. I'd like to have the nerve to tell the boss off or have that control over my life." In the society we live in, everything is kind of controlled for us. We just grow up and everything's kind of done. A lot of people are drawn to an original like Dirty Harry. The general public interpreted it on that level, a man concerned with a victim he'd never met. Like everybody says, "Boy, if I were the victim of violent crime, I'd sure like to have someone expend that kind of effort on my behalf." And I think a lot of people believe that there isn't anybody who's willing to expend that kind of effort if they were in that situation.

'There may not be. Right. That may be the fantasy – that there might be someone interested in my problem if I was ever in that spot. That preys on people's minds these days with crime in America, in the world. Jesus, is there somebody there, is there anybody there?'

Eastwood has looked after himself which of course is his great screen appeal. But it wasn't always easy simply to believe in himself.

'Everything that has been successful for me was done against advice to the contrary, including the motion-picture business to begin with. There are two types of actors – those who reach out to their audience and say, "Come, caress me," and the others who say, "Here I am. Watch me if you want." I'll give you an example from old-time actors. Kirk Douglas and Burt Lancaster were more reach-out: 'I'm coming down to the front row to see you. Sit back in your seats – pow!' A lot of power. Gary Cooper and Henry Fonda were more, "Lean forward, cause I'm going to be talking very quietly. You're gonna have to reach for what I'm gonna give you or you'd better just leave."

'If a character doesn't grow in each film, if he doesn't learn something about life as he goes along, there isn't any sense in doing the film. I think that women have changed, men have changed, too, and I hope for the better.'

Neither is it simple to explain his intimidating work ethic.

'I shoot fast. *Play Misty for Me* was wrapped in little over five weeks. *Breezy* was completed in less than five weeks. It's not just a matter of money, I like to have momentum, to keep the spirit and energy going. To me, directing is knowing the concept you want and getting it. Shooting on location is easier, because a crew gets wrapped up in the spirit of the film. I cast my crews as carefully as I cast my actors. That's why we have such happy, democratic crews. And we move – I try not to keep people on location too long.

'A director should change camera angles a lot. My theory is when you're looking at a film, you're looking at a flat piece projected on to a flat surface. The only way you can approach a 3-D feeling is to cross over and get the camera right in there so the audience can feel a part of a group rather than just observers of a group. Camera work is a lot like penmanship, the way you film a film says as much as the way it's written.

'Casting is one of the most important aspects in making a film. A film can live or die on it. The cast has to bring those characters to life. If you miscast a character, or one stands out strong, you can throw the whole picture out of whack. It's like having a pebble in your tire.

'People say I know just what the public wants. I don't think that people themselves know what they want until they see it or hear about it. One should judge a property [a potential film] simply by whether or not one would like to go see it. There's a lot of gut instinct going when buying or rejecting a property.

'A lot of critics thought *Dirty Harry* was sort of a right-wing film. It wasn't at all. It portrayed the circumstances that one guy was put into, and showed the frustration with our courts and our judicial system. Which is all very timely even today. The film was just ahead of itself. I try to say something different in every film and this one is about that frustration. *Play Misty for Me* was a little statement on commitment and misinterpreting commitment in men and women. There is not a Clint Eastwood message. There are lots of different messages.

'You learn from everyone you work with. I'm surrounded by the best crew around and we all like to move at the same tempo. I think if the director is slow and ponderous, it can hurt the final project. The movie might not be as satisfying and, besides I'd get bored. My sanity would not have lasted through *Heaven's Gate*. I'm a little more patient than I used to be, but not that patient.

'In recent years I have learned to look at films and I like films a lot better. There is something about the whole film-making process that has been more important to me. As a young actor, it was different because you only cared about the overall production. That is a different thing. I have dreams to do more films. More expansive roles. As I get older, I fit more roles. Hopefully, I will be able to broaden the spectrum.

'I have my own production company. I'll probably keep that going for a long time. I have been very, very lucky to have gotten into a position where I can sort of control my destiny, so to speak; to do the kind of things I want to do. That is a dream to me and that's more important than any monetary compensation. It's an old game to say you can make a picture for such and such when you know darned well you can't, and then your financiers are vulnerable. I don't play that game. I give the financiers respect – and I demand it in return. If they don't know it, they shouldn't be hiring me. I don't know all the answers. But I don't know anyone who does.

'You do need a great deal of patience to direct any sort of film. I'm sure I was less tolerant when I was younger. Although I don't think I've ever been regarded as a difficult actor to work with. I always try to be reasonably sensitive to other people's needs.

'I'm never looking for any particular type of script – they just come about. I think I've been lucky. If I had sat down and planned it that way, I probably wouldn't have planned it any better. You do things as best you can. I've always had a philosophy, I guess, I try to get as much on the screen for the money as possible. I treat the audience as having the same IQ as myself.

'I was raised with films that had a lot of action, with Gary Cooper and John Wayne and stuff. And people are interested in action in films. Action and drama and conflict seem to be the motivating force for a lot of entertainment. I like romantic films but it's easier said than done. It's so hard to find material. There's a certain element of the public who like those Dirty Harry roles and it's a great male fantasy kind of character, but I think you can only do that so much in life and then eventually you want to branch out and do other things, and I've done other things in between.

'I think Westerns are a great form of entertainment and maybe it's a chance doing one. I never know. I don't think so. I think the public will go for it if it's any good. That's the way I felt about it all along – just because I'm in it isn't gonna help. If it's not a good film then the public doesn't feel rewarded in some way when they leave the cinema.

'You try to treat people well because they're treating you well. They're going to your films. I don't have much respect for people who look down on the public as somebody that gets in the way. After all, you asked for it, you fought to get where you are – on the other hand, you want privacy too because otherwise if people can use you up to a point, your central nervous system goes berserk. In fact, you just do the best you can. To me, I'm still only interested in work.'

But how do you do the best work? How does *he* do his best work?

'I think every actor has a different way of getting to the same result and there's no set formula. Some people like to go bang their head against the wall to cry and other people sit there and think about their puppy that was run over when they were ten years old. Some people just think of the situation at hand whatever it is. Whatever way it gets you is the way there. All you're trying to do is affect the audience and make them believe that you're believable. Acting is more than ranting and raving and rolling around on the floor. I've always felt that a full barrel makes a lot less noise than an empty one. Still waters run deep.

'I always feel a responsibility to do the best I can for the people who are putting money up. But at the same time, I have to do it the way I believe. You can't try to make your film based on what people may want. I don't think studio executives are always happy to hear what I want to do. You should have heard the arguments I made to get them to let me do *Play Misty for Me*. "Who the hell wants to see Clint Eastwood play a disc jockey?" I said: "Well, who the hell wants to see me do anything?" It's good for me, and it's good for them to try other things. If I'd stayed in the Western genre I don't think I'd still be around. I don't think I'd ever have been able to do *Escape from Alcatraz* or *Bronco Billy* or *Honkytonk Man*. I wouldn't have been able to branch out into directing. People get tired of seeing you do the same thing.

'Some people don't want you to take that big swing. It's just not what they expect or want from you. But I can't let that stop me.

If you think about that, you're going to make decisions for all the wrong reasons. If you don't take some chances, why do it?

'When I was going over the material for *Sudden Impact* with the screenwriter I came to the line, "Go ahead, make my day." I said, "This is really good," I knew it would click. But how! One lady hired an airplane to tow a banner saying, "Clint, make my day," signed Kathy or whatever it was. It was just crazy. But it hasn't changed any. It's everywhere I go.

'If you start thinking about the end results and start anticipating what an audience might feel, you may be dead wrong. I just go ahead with my way and figure that at least I can have the satisfaction of having put it down. And if it works, it works, and if it doesn't, move on. You have to put personal relationships aside. You have to be selfish about who you use in a picture. You use people you think can do the job. You can't just let your mind be ruled by other feelings.'

Eastwood then emphasizes his admiration for Action Women and Men: 'I've always felt that the more a woman is active in life, same as a man, the more interesting she is to be around. There's no reason women shouldn't try to attain everything they're capable of. During the seventies we had to pigeonhole everybody in some category – either sexist or racist or chauvinist or whatever-you-call-ist. That was an unhealthy period, and I'm glad it's over. A lot of other films I've done appeal to fantasies. The romance of the individual who says and does the right thing at the right time is very strong. As women become more involved with careers, they understand better the kind of Mickey Mouse bureaucracies the characters I play are always fighting against. But I think women still find a man they can rely on appealing. I don't think the roles have changed that much.

'Most people who get to a certain stage in making movies usually are the best at what they do. In other words, they do things that nobody else can do. There's a lot of other actors that do more variety, but no specific thing that is them. You can say that about Cary Grant, John Wayne. Whatever they did, they did it and nobody else could do it. People would try to imitate them over the years and nobody could imitate them. Most actors don't work that way, don't work in reserve, because it's a hard thing to do.

'Gary Cooper, when he was asked to explain his acting technique, used to say that he was just thinking hard what his next line was. George Cukor used to get great results from Garbo by telling her to think of nothing in the close-ups. Obviously, her thinking of nothing was more interesting than another girl thinking of a lot of things.

'Macho is probably one of the most misused words in the language. Over the years, I think the most macho guys on the screen were also very sensitive people. I think Bogart and Cagney and Wayne could all portray great sensitivity. The truth is that strong men are sensitive and aren't afraid of showing it. It's the people that are insecure about their manliness, who are adverse about showing their feelings, who have to do that cock-of-the-walk, strut-your-stuff kind of thing. And it's the people who take man pills and have to go around kicking over furniture all the time who are usually insecure about their manliness. Just like a woman who has to go around acting twitty all the time, flirting and chirping like a canary. A woman like that may be insecure about her femininity. Femininity is an inner thing – it's that simple. A woman doesn't have to be a centrefold to be beautiful. She could even have a low voice like Katharine Hepburn's. This culture has too many clichés and stereotypes.'

But clichés and stereotypes aside, Eastwood has enjoyed magic moments, the good, the bad and the ugly of movie-making.

'This has been a great era for actors. Any actor who's doing well can have a certain amount of control. In the old days, it was, "Here's your next picture, Mr Bogart." Today, you're a free agent. So I pick things that jump off the page at me.

'Cary Grant never won the Academy Award. He was a brilliant comedian. People didn't understand how brilliant he was. One of the great entertainers of our lifetime. Not that he needed it, he probably didn't care.

'I remember going to a party when I was a young contract player at Universal. Someone introduced me to Cornel Wilde. I'd never met a movie star. I didn't know any celebrities. Cornel Wilde was in his heyday then. He said to me: "Save your money." I said: "I don't have any money." He said: "If you get any money, save it. That way you won't have to do projects just for the sake of existing." I gather he was talking about himself. Perhaps he felt he had done a lot of movies he shouldn't have done. I've always remembered that advice. A lot of it is luck, but if you manage yourself well, you can step back if things aren't right.'

Eastwood then argued about the violence of his films against the reality of violence. His heart today certainly sounds as though it is hovering around the less commercial films he makes.

'Everybody's trying to break the bank or make a $100 million film. Everybody's looking for the road to commercial success. I've had a certain amount of commercial success along the way, so I'm just looking to make some good stories. Rigidity is death and flexibility is birth. God gave you a brain to think, and if you don't use it, it's going to get rigid, and it's going to get smaller, until it's just a tiny pea inside your skull. I think the directing personality is just being able to lead the platoon up the hill and the acting personality is, OK, what are we going to shoot at on the way to protect ourselves? It's a life of escapism. Maybe that's why so many actors get screwed up along the way. They tend to rely on the escapist part rather than the reality part. I think I've always been a realist. Your brain can go fast. After a while you forget that you once bagged groceries or worked in a gas station or dug ditches.

'When we were kids, we thought if you kill somebody, they electrocute you. Jimmy Cagney, the big house, the chair, zzzzz, you're dead. Nowadays, it's not that way. One guy gets thirty years for robbery, another gets six for murder. If there's irresponsibility in *Dirty Harry*, there's irresponsibility in Robin Hood, Tom Mix, and the Old Testament. There is violence in all of them. I don't advocate violence, I never have. I don't enjoy arbitrary violence, and I think hunting animals is disgusting.

'Everybody has certain reservations about violence. I don't mind sexy movies and I don't mind violent movies, but I don't like sex and violence together. That bothers me. But what relationship violence has to society, I don't know. I don't know which is imitative of which. I think movie violence is a convenient fall guy. When you haven't got anything else to blame, blame it on that. My generation grew up watching Paul Muni, George Raft, Humphrey Bogart and James Cagney blowing people away, and it didn't make us criminals – I'm not sure it does today. People have to monitor what their kids see. I guess that's what the rating system's all about.

'I tell you kids are amazing. Adults always have the greatest fears about kids and probably justifiably so, but kids know a lot more than most adults think they know and with the violence thing I've never had to explain much to them. We'll see a movie together and maybe the movie is in poor taste and then we'll discuss it.

'I'm against war period. When I was in the army, I was against the Korean War, and after that – although I wasn't a protester – I was against Vietnam. But people want to see reality in movies, and the world is a violent place. It's nothing new. Being killed with a gun is probably better than being hacked to death with a sword, the way they did it in medieval times. People want to see crooks being punished hard. They see the cops losing the battle for law and order. There is a wave of feeling in America among people who have had it up to here with violence on the streets. The trend in our country now is to weight scales in favour of the criminal.

'My sympathy has always been with the victim. Not that I'm against the rights of the accused. Every effort must be made to see that a person is never prosecuted for something he didn't do. At the same time, I worry about people who are at risk.'

And there you have the dichotomy of the Eastwood image. Dirty Harry vs. Zubin Mehta, Josey Wales vs. Dave Brubeck – he's against injustice and pro the arts.

'I like art and I like music very much. I used to play flute, cornet, and piano when I was a kid. In fact, I wanted to go to the University of Seattle Music School but, unfortunately, I procrastinated and got inducted into the service so I had to abandon that idea. I fiddle around on the piano – mostly writing things. I have composed music for three or four films. I am not a well-schooled musician, but I have loved music all my life. I am surprised that I never got into it.

'Any art enriches one's life, you bet. I don't collect any particular art or artist, but I have a lot of various pieces. I have Remington, Russell, some of the newer Western art people. I have Michael Coleman, people like that, but I also have Rockwell. I have all kinds of things; I'm not glued to one particular style.

'When I worked for a timber company in Springfield, near Eugene, Oregon, and all they played up there was country music – Hank Snow and all that kind of stuff – I never liked it. I always preferred jazz. I'd stay up all night so I could listen to Jimmy Lyons broadcasting from San Francisco at midnight, playing the hot stuff at the time – Brubeck and Mulligan and all that. My mother had a collection of Fats Waller records, and she played the piano and taught me. Later on I became interested in the self-destruct kind of country guys – Hank Williams, Red Foley – after I read *Honkytonk Man*. I appreciate it more now than I did as a kid. I like rhythm and blues and pop. I thought rock 'n' roll by white guys was boring – sounded like guys trying to be black and didn't have it.

'There are two American art forms, the Western and jazz. It's funny how Americans don't support either of them any more. My Westerns are the way they are because of the point in history where I picked it up. John Wayne once wrote me a letter, and he wasn't very pleased about *High Plains Drifter*. He said that isn't what the West was all about, that isn't the American people who settled this country. I said: "You're absolutely right." It's just an allegory, and it wasn't intended to be the West that's been told hundreds of times over by many players, about pioneers and covered wagons and conflict with the various Indian nations. *High Plains Drifter* was a speculation on what happens when they go ahead and kill the sheriff and somebody comes back and calls the town's conscience to bear. There's always retribution for your deeds.'

—

ELEVEN

Walk Tall

'I don't think Clint will ever hang up his guns. He'll go out blazing.'

SAM BOTTOMS, ACTOR, ON CLINT EASTWOOD

Although he is adamant he will not get into national politics, Eastwood has given his support to environmental causes. In 1990 he did a series of television commercials along with Ted Danson of television's *Cheers* and Kyle Mac-Lachlan and Michael Ontkean of *Twin Peaks* to support legislation to stop clear-cutting in California's forests. Environmental groups were delighted to recruit Eastwood who showed he was a conservationist as well as a conservative. Eastwood urged voters to 'save the last five per cent of California's redwoods'.

His involvement provoked more talk of him running for political office. He was said to look the part. He dismissed the notion: 'If I've got a presidential face I'm lacking in a lot of other areas.' Eastwood kept his word. By 1992 he was investing in the environment along with Jack Nicholson and Sylvester Stallone. Stallone owns eleven acres and has an option on twenty acres more no-glitz opposite to star-studded Aspen, the flashy ski resort where you can lie on the snow and watch stars and vice versa. But you can lie on the snow and watch stars and vice versa. But Telluride residents and regular visitors fear that Stallone's involvement will turn their small town into a boom town. The last time the folks there got so upset was when Butch Cassidy rode in and pulled off his first bank robbery in 1889.

But Stallone along with Eastwood, Nicholson and other investors were attempting to buy 160 acres of mountain slopes and forests around Telluride in the spring of 1992 for both commercial and environmental reasons. The people of Telluride were not in the least excited about the prospect of commercial development. Stallone was already the biggest landowner and has sold his 23-acre ranch in Hidden Valley, California for $4 million. At Hidden Valley he had a jacuzzi bath for his horses and it is that sort of Hollywood flamboyance which concerns the more down to earth Telluride townspeople. The town welcomes visitors but on equal terms. And they must play by town rules. The Silver Globe restaurant turned away tycoon Donald Trump who wanted to pay by credit card not cash. Arnold Schwarzenegger was jeered by other customers at a ski-slope cafe when he did not clear away his table as is the custom.

Eastwood, as is his style, has not been a high visibility investor. He believes that by being part of the project he can be an influence against exploitation of this particular section of the Rocky Mountains. Stallone has been the one in the firing line. He is an intimidating presence in town with his four bodyguards and two pitbull terriers. The dogs are called Oscar after the comedy film which didn't win him one and Adrienne, the name of his wife played by Talia Shire in the *Rocky* films. He is also intimidating on the slopes. He had a run-in with ski-lift attendant Ed Setton whom Stallone did not treat with the usual courtesy of saying hello. Setton, out of Stallone's hearing, reportedly called the star 'a jerk'. A Stallone bodyguard heard the remark and the next day Stallone approached Setton. It is said that foul words were shouted at Setton by the Stallone group and one of them told Setton: 'We'll have your job.'

Setton was indeed fired from his job and the people of Telluride were furious, convinced the ski company was trying to keep Stallone happy because of future investments. They started such a stink that a compromise was made: Setton was suspended for two weeks and then returned to a different lift than the one used by Stallone and Co.

Meanwhile, Eastwood was interested in cinema showdowns. With all the outside pressures and the time on African location for *White Hunter, Black Heart*, 1991 became only the third year in the previous fifteen years that Warner Brothers did not have a Clint Eastwood film on its summer or Christmas schedule.

In September 1991, Eastwood's latest showdown was starting. He and his loyal band of film-makers were in Alberta, Canada, to make *Unforgiven*. The period Western – his first since

Pale Rider in 1985 – was filmed in the hamlets of Brooks, Drumheller, Stettler and Longview and also at rodeos in Calgary and in Sonora, Arizona, on the Mexican border. It is vintage Eastwood and he was clearly set on making a classic Western like *The Outlaw Josey Wales* in 1976. The script for the film was titled *The William Munny Killings* and had been going the rounds in Hollywood for fifteen years. Writer David Peoples completed it in 1976. But although *Josey Wales* had been successful, other impressive Westerns like *The Culpepper Cattle Co.* and *The Great Northfield Minnesota Raid*, made in the early seventies, had not done well at the box office. The genre was in a slump and Peoples whose first screen credit was British director Ridley Scott's *Blade Runner* says: 'Nobody wanted to see Westerns. I didn't write it as a smart movie but it's worked out now.'

People's script was originally called *The Cut-Whore Killings* and director Francis Ford Coppola bought an option on the rights in the early 1980s but no studios were interested. Eastwood picked up the rights when Coppola's option ran out and had planned to make the film before the multiple Oscar success of Kevin Costner's *Dances With Wolves*. He believes Costner's success will not help or hinder his film – but it did prove to doubting Hollywood that there is a market for good Westerns. 'Everybody wants to pronounce genres dead then somebody comes along with a new twist and changes everything,' says Eastwood adding: 'The audience changes. There's a whole new generation out there.'

Indeed. In *Unforgiven* Eastwood stars as William Munny, a former convict and outlaw who has become a homesteader. He leaves his family to try for the $1000 bounty placed on a man who cut-up a prostitute. Morgan Freeman co-stars as Munny's side-kick, another reformed gunman. Gene Hackman is the sheriff who gets in the way of the bounty hunters and Richard Harris is English Bob, a hired gun and a particularly nasty piece of work. It is a stellar cast and Eastwood believes his forty-ninth film is a winner. When he makes his half-century, his fiftieth film, it will be one for him. It will be a romance.

. . .

It is no surprise that Eastwood intends to make a full-blown romantic film in 1993. It is the one genre which he has not explored. There was the knockabout comedy romance of *Every Which Way But Loose* and *Bronco Billy* but missing is the Eastwood approach to straightforward romantic drama. Or, more likely, convoluted romantic drama because that's the nature of that particular film form.

He's arguably the Last Great Hollywood star. His involvement in any project doesn't automatically make it an all-round success but it gives it immediate authority. And that's what he is today. An authority figure. A serious man who likes his secrets to remain secret. There is a touch of fatalism about him and also much humour. In his films he can be a romantic albeit a guilty one.

The first sign of that was in 1973 when he directed the late William Holden and Kay Lenz in *Breezy*. The late Joe Heims who also wrote *Play Misty for Me* was an influential Eastwood friend and he says of her: 'She wrote the man and the woman's characters so well I thought: I don't know if I'm going to act in it but I'd sure like to make it. I liked the whole comment of the rejuvenation of a cynic living around Los Angeles, divorced, making good dough but hating it and then finding out about life through a seventeen year old. She teaches him more about it than he teaches her. It's a mutual exchange but it doesn't go on for ever and she doesn't die of some exotic disease.'

Breezy cost $275,000 to make. In the summer of 1992 scripts for a romantic drama were being written for Eastwood with film budgets possible at certainly ten if not twenty times that amount of money. He then planned to take on his roles of producer and director. Whether he would also star was then dependent on the story. There was no question that, at sixty-two, he still looked the part of a romantic leading man. Man Watchers Incorporated, a 15,000-member American organization, voted him 'a dreamboat' in the summer of 1992 and president Suzy Mallery reported: 'He's still in shape – an example of the fact that you don't get older, you get better.'

But one sensed that Eastwood was tidying up loose ends, putting his house in order. His life has been an astonishing series of successful cycles; he has never gone out of fashion but that, of course, is because he has never been universally 'in', except at the box office. He convinced his daughter Alison to pursue her college education. He spent more than $1 million on a home in the Hollywood Hills for Kyle who in the summer of 1992 was becoming a recognized musician. The house has five bedrooms, a maid's quarters and a large music room in 4,500 square feet. The second floor comprises the master bedroom. It was totally redecorated before Kyle moved in: altogether a lavish reward for his son's love – and loyalty. There is never any talk or comment now about Sondra Locke. He still is in close touch with Maggie Eastwood – they remain Carmel neighbours – and he is enjoying his stature as an American icon.

Mature. Mellower. All those years of laying the foundations, from digging swimming pools to his roles in B Westerns, have paid off handsomely. He says he wants to do more 'expansive' things but the days of film-making in power-punching, one-two-three, thank you ma'm, style are over. His kids are grown and other affairs cleared up: he's liked things tidy since his army days and even where there were still some emotional knots in the summer of 1992, the practical matters were neatly arranged.

When legendary American talk-show host Johnny Carson ended his thirty-year run on television that summer one of his last guests was Eastwood who for years had always been wary of being 'bushwhacked' by difficult questions on live television. But he didn't just appear with Carson – he went off to have dinner with him at La Scala in Malibu after the show.

It was in the American Midwest not La Scala in Milan where Eastwood was inducted into the American Music Hall of Fame for his love of jazz and his film *Bird*. He was still very proud. 'I always felt sorry for younger people who didn't grow up in the swinging generation,' he laughingly told a cheering crowd of 5000 at the Chevron Jazz Festival in Moscow, Idaho. But these days Eastwood is more likely to be found in Washington or Hollywood or Beverly Hills at some major charity event than in the American Midwest where he remains one of the most popular stars. He's gone from poncho to black tie. At the Los Angeles Armand Hammer Museum he turned out with First Lady Barbara Bush, Gregory Peck and Kevin Costner to raise money.

When he walks into the room, he knows at least two people will say: 'Go ahead, make my day!' as they ask for an autograph. And at least one woman will slip him a phone number with a similar comment. Something along the lines of how she could make his day. He has heard all the lines. But you would never know it. The fans usually get their autographs these days, the women get a friendly smile. If he likes what he's looking at the smile simply gets broader and warmer.

He has matured into a self-effacing but powerful force in Hollywood, in the cinema world-wide. Up on the screen he's larger than life. Off-screen he walks about with similar confidence. Alan Murray who has been the sound effects editor on a string of Eastwood films found that image a problem:

> *You can't have him hit somebody and make it sound like a slap – you've got to hear the bones break in the guy's jaw. You try to match the sound to the character. When he's mad, I will make the gunshot louder than when he's running down a street and shooting at somebody.*

The big challenge was always to give him a walk as impressive as his persona. It was difficult to get the right walk for Clint. I must have gone through ten pairs of shoes. Finally, I looked in a closet and found these shoes my father had worn in the Forties. They had very hard leather soles with a bit of wood in between. And we tried these and it was Clint's walk. It had weight, it had manliness and strength to it.

Actor George Dzundza who worked for him on *White Hunter, Black Heart* and played Michael Douglas' police partner in the 1992 sex thriller *Basic Instinct* makes this point: 'You sense a sort of gentility, a sort of man's approach to things.' And that's one of the reasons why Eastwood rather than any other star – or celebrity image – is conjured up in messages from the White House to Gulf War campaigns to reflect a cool, calm but certainly effective way of taking care of business. Any sort of business.

Before New York 'Godfather' John Gotti was convicted of racketeering and murder charges in the spring of 1992, the Oscar-winning actor Anthony Quinn appeared in court escorted to his seat by some Gotti henchmen. 'I came because I want to make a picture about this drama.' Quinn recalled knowing Benjamin 'Bugsy' Siegel and gangster Frank Costello. The veteran actor said he wanted to play mobster Paul Castenello whose murder formed a major part of the Gotti trial. US Attorney Andrew Maloney was clearly angered by the glorification of the proceedings and the presence of Mr Quinn. He smiled: 'Next week, we're going to bring Clint Eastwood.'

For all the critics, all the bile over violence and *Dirty Harry*, Eastwood has emerged in the autumn of his career as an instant image. He's Mr Good. Mr Right. The Pale Rider. Like Sean Connery he has the major gift of *always* looking comfortable no matter what role he is publicly playing. The difficult times have been as husband and lover, the times, we might say, when he was looking at the wrong end of a .44 magnum.

He's a fascinating man. He's concerned about abused kids and the abused planet. He'll stop on the road driving through Arizona or Mexico to rescue an injured iguana. He bottle-feeds lambs on his ranch – even when he isn't running for political office – but seems strangely remote and unable to commit fully to human relationships. Could it be that he's simply a man born to be a bachelor? He enjoys women. But he also enjoys cars, motorbikes, playing pool, hanging out in bars and jazz clubs, camping, skiing, golfing, riding and pumping iron. One of the boys, eh?

'I can cook and clean and I've been known to make a few beds,' he says of his independence. He says he has lots of women 'friends' but he doesn't think he will get married again. That is a subject that, in the right mood, will have him playfully gasping and clutching his throat. Yes, he says, he could retire but that's not on the horizon, there's no crimson sunset he plans to ride into. He pulls a fact out of the air. Men don't live as long as women. Therefore? They have to take advantages faster.' He learned that growing up during the Depression. He was a loner then. And he remains one today. Content? Probably. Happy? Could be? Retiring? Never.

One of his friends in Carmel told me in the summer over a chat about politics and the merits of President George Bush, Democratic candidate Governor Bill Clinton and the multi-millionaire wild card Ross Perot: 'You look at it on paper and Clint could take any of them in the polls.'

Would he ever try politics again?

'Maybe,' was the answer.

And you had to recall actor Sam Bottoms talking about Eastwood on the set of *Bronco Billy*. Bottoms who also appeared in *The Outlaw Josey Wales* observed: 'I don't think Clint will ever hang up his guns. He'll go out blazing.' Which is where he – and we – came in.

Filmography

C lint Eastwood played Rowdy Yates in *Rawhide* from 1958 to 1966. The series began being shown on American television on 9 January 1959, with the episode 'Incident of the Tumbleweed Wagon'. Frankie Laine who sang the theme song was a guest star in a 1960 episode titled 'Incident on the Road to Yesterday'.

Many remarkable names appeared on the series including: Charles Bronson, Troy Donahue, Brian Donlevy, Martha Hyer, MacDonald Carey, Leslie Nielsen, Gary Merrill, Dan Duryea, Linda Cristal, Brian Keith, Victor McLaglen, Patricia Medina, Vera Miles, John Drew Barrymore, Cesar Romero, Neville Brand, Jock Mahoney, Buddy Ebsen, Julie London, Robert Cotte, Peter Lorre, Dan O'Herlihy, Agnes Moorhead, Mercedes Mc-Cambridge, Woody Strode, Mary Astor, Robert Culp, John Cassavetes, Jack Lord, Richard Basehart, Charles Gray, Zachary Scott, Barbara Stanwyck, James Coburn, Walter Pidgeon, John Ireland, Claude Rains, Burgess Meredith, Bill Travers, Frankie Avalon, Mickey Rooney, Warren Oates, Dean Martin, Lee Van Cleef, Louis Hayward, Nick Adams, Pat Hingle, Robert Blake, Steve Forrest, Eddie Albert, Julie Harris, Efrem Zimbalist, Jr., Claude Atkins, Ralph Bellamy, Forest Tucker and Denver Pyle. Many of the *Rawhide* guest stars would go on to appear in Eastwood films over the years. He had a memory. He was loyal.

Eastwood made ten films before the series began and during it made *A Fistful of Dollars* in 1964. Here all the Eastwood movies:

REVENGE OF THE CREATURE, Universal-International, USA, 1955
Director: Jack Arnold
John Agar (Clete Ferguson), Lori Nelson (Helen Dobson), Clint Eastwood (uncredited as Jennings a lab technician).

TARANTULA, Universal-International, USA, 1955

Director: Jack Arnold
John Agar (Dr. Matt Hastings), Leo G. Carroll (Prof. Deemer), Clint Eastwood (uncredited as a bomber pilot).

LADY GODIVA OF COVENTRY, Universal-International, USA, 1955
Director: Arthur Lubin
Maureen O'Hara (Lady Godiva), George Nader (Lord Leofic), Clint Eastwood (First Saxon).

FRANCIS IN THE NAVY, Universal-International, USA, 1955
Director: Arthur Lubin
Donald O'Connor (Lt Peter Stirling), Martha Hyer (Betsy Donevan), Jim Backus (Commander Hutch), Clint Eastwood (Jonesy), Chill Wills (voice of Francis).

NEVER SAY GOODBYE, Universal-International, USA, 1955
Director: Jerry Hopper
Rock Hudson (Dr Michael Parker), George Sanders (Victor), Shelley Fabares (Suzy Parker), Clint Eastwood (Will).

THE FIRST TRAVELING SALESLADY, RKO-Radio, USA, 1956
Director: Arthur Lubin
Ginger Rogers (Rose Gillray), Carol Channing (Molly Wade), James Arness (Joel Kingdom), Clint Eastwood (Jack Rice).

STAR IN THE DUST, Universal-International, USA, 1956
Director: Charles Haas
John Agar (Bill Jordan), Mamie Van Doren (Ellen Ballard), Richard Boone (Sam Hall), Leif Erikson (George Ballard), Clint Eastwood (uncredited as a ranch hand).

ESCAPADE IN JAPAN, RKO-Radio, USA, 1957
Director: Arthur Lubin
Teresa Wright (Mary Saunders), Cameron Mitchell (Dick Saunders), Clint Eastwood (uncredited as a rescue pilot One Dumbo).

LAFAYETTE ESCADRILLE, Warner Brothers, USA, 1958
Director: William A. Wellman
Tab Hunter (Thad Walker), David Janssen (Duke Sinclair), Clint Eastwood (George Moseley). British title: Hell Bent for Glory.

AMBUSH AT CIMARRON PASS, 20th Century Fox, USA, 1958
Director: Jodie Copeland
Scott Brady (Sgt Matt Blake), Clint Eastwood (Keith Williams).

A FISTFUL OF DOLLARS, United Artists, Italy/West Germany/Spain, 1964
Director: Sergio Leone
Clint Eastwood (The Stranger), John Welles [Gian Maria Volonte] (Ramon Rojo), Marianne Koch (Marisol).

FOR A FEW DOLLARS MORE, United Artists, Italy/Spain/ West Germany, 1965
Director: Sergio Leone
Clint Eastwood (The Stranger), Lee Van Cleef (Colonel Mortimer), Klaus Kinski (Hunchback).

THE GOOD, THE BAD AND THE UGLY, United Artists, Italy, 1966
Director: Sergio Leone
Clint Eastwood (Joe), Eli Wallach (Tuco), Lee Van Cleef (Setenza).

THE WITCHES, United Artists, Italy/France, 1966
Directors: Luchino Visconti (pt 1)
Mauro Bolognini (pt 2)
Piero Paolo Pasolini (pt 3)
Franco Rossi (pt 4)
Vittorio De Sica (pt 5)
Silvano Mangano (Giovanna), Clint Eastwood (Mario, Mangano's husband).

HANG 'EM HIGH, United Artists, USA, 1967
Director: Ted Post
Clint Eastwood (Jed Cooper), Inger Stevens (Rachel), Ed Begley (Captain Wilson), Pat Hingle (Judge Adam Fenton), James MacArthur (Priest).

COOGAN'S BLUFF, Universal, USA, 1968
Director: Don Siegel
Clint Eastwood (Walt Coogan), Lee J. Cobb (McElroy), Susan Clark (Julie), Don Stroud (Ringerman).

WHERE EAGLES DARE, MGM, Great Britain, 1968
Director: Brian G. Hutton
Richard Burton (John Smith), Clint Eastwood (Lt Morris Schaffer), Mary Ure (Mary Ellison), Patrick Wymark (Colonel Turner), Michael Hordern (Vice-Admiral Rolland), Donald Houston (Christiansen), Peter Barkworth (Berkeley), Robert Beatty (Cartwright Jones), Anton Diffring (Colonel Kramer), Ferdy Mayne (Reichsmarschal Rosemeyer), Ingrid Pitt (Heidi).

PAINT YOUR WAGON, Paramount, USA, 1969
Director: Joshua Logan
Lee Marvin (Ben Rumson), Clint Eastwood (Pardner), Jean Seberg (Elizabeth), Harve Presnell (Rotten Luck Willie).

TWO MULES FOR SISTER SARA, Universal/Malpaso, USA
1969
Director: Don Siegel
Shirley MacLaine (Sara), Clint Eastwood (Hogan).

KELLY'S HEROES, MGM-EMI, USA/Yugoslavia, 1970
Director: Brian G. Hutton
Clint Eastwood (Kelly), Telly Savalas (Big Joe), Don Rickles
(Crapgame), Donald Sutherland (Oddball), Carroll O'Connor
(Gen. Colt).

THE BEGUILED, Universal/Malpasa, USA, 1971
Director: Don Siegel
Clint Eastwood (John McBurney), Geraldine Page (Martha
Farnsworth), Elizabeth Hartman (Edwina Dabney).

PLAY MISTY FOR ME, Universal/Malpaso, USA, 1971
Director: Clint Eastwood
Clint Eastwood (Dave Garland), Jessica Walter (Evelyn Draper),
Donna Mills (Tobie Williams).

DIRTY HARRY, Columbia-Warner, USA, 1971
Director: Don Siegel
Clint Eastwood (Harry Callahan), Harry Guardino (Lt
Bressler), Reni Santoni (Chico), John Vernon (The Mayor),
Andy Robinson (Scorpio).

JOE KIDD, Universal/Malpaso, USA, 1972
Director: John Sturges
Clint Eastwood (Joe Kidd), Robert Duvall (Frank Harlan), John
Saxon (Luis Chama), Don Stroud (Lamarr).

HIGH PLAINS DRIFTER, Universal/Malpaso, USA, 1972
Director: Clint Eastwood
Clint Eastwood (The Stranger), Verna Bloom (Sarah Belding),
Mariana Hill (Callie Trevors), Mitchell Ryan (Dave Drake).

BREEZY, Universal/Malpaso, USA, 1973
Director: Clint Eastwood
William Holden (Frank Harmon), Kay Lenz (Breezy).

MAGNUM FORCE, Malpaso, USA, 1973
Director: Ted Post
Clint Eastwood (Inspector Harry Callahan), Hal Holbrook
(Lieutenant Neil Briggs), Mitchell Ryan (Charlie McCoy),
David Soul (Ben David), Robert Urich (John Grimes).

THUNDERBOLT AND LIGHTFOOT, Malpaso Company, USA,
1974
Director: Michael Cimino
Clint Eastwood (John 'Thunderbolt' Doherty), Jeff Bridges
(Lightfoot), George Kennedy (Red Leary), Geoffrey Lewis
(Goody), Catherine Bach (Melody), Gary Busey (Curly).

THE EIGER SANCTION, Universal/Malpaso Company, USA,
1975
Director: Clint Eastwood
Clint Eastwood (Johnathan Hemlock), George Kennedy (Ben
Bowman), Vonetta McGee (Jemima Brown), Jack Cassidy (Miles
McHough), Brenda Venus (George).

THE OUTLAW JOSEY WALES, Malpaso for Warner Brothers,
USA, 1976
Director: Clint Eastwood
Clint Eastwood (Josey Wales), Chief Dan George (Lone Watie),
Sondra Locke (Laura Lee), Bill McKinney (Terrill), John
Vernon (Fletcher), Sam Bottoms (Jamie).

THE ENFORCER, Malpaso for Warner Brothers, USA, 1976
Director: James Fargo
Clint Eastwood (Inspector Harry Callahan), Harry Guardino
(Lt Bressler), Bradford Dillman (Capt. McKay), Tyne Daly
(Kate Moore).

THE GAUNTLET, Malpaso for Warner Brothers, USA, 1977
Director: Clint Eastwood
Clint Eastwood (Ben Shockley), Sondra Locke (Gus Mally), Pat
Hingle (Josephson), William Prince (Blakelock).

EVERY WHICH WAY BUT LOOSE, Malpaso for Warner
Brothers, USA, 1978
Director: James Fargo
Clint Eastwood (Philo Beddoe), Sondra Locke (Lynn Halsey-
Taylor), Ruth Gordon (Ma), Geoffrey Lewis (Orville), Beverly
D'Angelo (Echo).

ESCAPE FROM ALCATRAZ, Malpaso for Paramount, USA,
1979
Director: Don Siegel
Clint Eastwood (Frank Morris), Patrick McGoohan (Warden).

BRONCO BILLY, Warner Brothers, USA, 1980
Director: Clint Eastwood
Clint Eastwood ('Bronco Billy' McCoy), Sondra Locke
(Antoinette Lily), Geoffrey Lewis (John Arlington), Scatman
Crothers ('Doc' Lynch), Sam Bottoms (Leonard James), Sierra
Pecheur (Lorraine Running Water).

ANY WHICH WAY YOU CAN, Malpaso for Warner Brothers,
USA, 1980
Director: Buddy Van Horn

Clint Eastwood (Philo Beddoe), Sondra Locke (Lynn Halsey-Taylor), Geoffrey Lewis (Orville Boggs), William Smith (Jack Wilson), Harry Guardino (James Beekman), Ruth Gordon (Ma Boggs).

HONKYTONK MAN, Malpaso for Warner Brothers, USA, 1982
Director: Clint Eastwood
Clint Eastwood (Red Stovall), Kyle Eastwood (Whit), John McIntire (Grandpa), Verna Bloom (Emmy).

FIREFOX, Malpaso for Warner Brothers, USA, 1982
Director: Clint Eastwood
Clint Eastwood (Mitchell Gant), Freddie Jones (Kenneth Aubrey), Ronald Lacey (Semelovsky).

SUDDEN IMPACT, Malpaso for Warner Brothers, USA, 1983
Director: Clint Eastwood
Clint Eastwood (Harry Callahan), Sondra Locke (Jennifer Spencer), Pat Hingle (Chief Jannings), Bradford Dillman (Captain Griggs).

TIGHTROPE, Warner Brothers A Malpaso Production, USA, 1984
Director: Richard Tuggle
Clint Eastwood (Wes Block), Genevieve Bujold (Beryl Thibodeaux), Dan Hedaya (Detective Molinari), Alison Eastwood (Amanda Block), Jennifer Beck (Penny Block).

CITY HEAT, Malpaso/Deliverance for Warner Brothers, USA, 1984
Director: Richard Benjamin
Clint Eastwood (Lieutenant Speer), Burt Reynolds (Mike Murphy), Jane Alexander (Addy), Madeline Kahn (Caroline

Howley), Rip Torn (Primo Pitt), Irene Cara (Ginny Lee),
Richard Roundtree (Dehl Swift), Tony Lo Bianco (Leon Coll).

PALE RIDER, Warner Brothers A Malpaso Production, USA,
1985
Director: Clint Eastwood
Clint Eastwood (Preacher), Michael Moriarty (Hull Barret),
Carrie Snodgress (Sarah Wheeler), Christopher Penn (Josh
LaHood), Richard Dysart (Coy LaHood), Richard Kiel (Club),
John Russell (Marshal Stockburn).

VANESSA IN THE GARDEN (TV episode for Steven
Spielberg's *Amazing Stories*), USA, 1985
Director: Clint Eastwood
Sondra Locke (Vanessa), Harvy Kitel and Beau Bridges.

HEARTBREAK RIDGE, Malpaso for Warner Brothers, USA,
1986
Director: Clint Eastwood
Clint Eastwood (Sergeant Thomas Highway), Marsha Mason
(Aggie), Everett McGill (Major Powers), Moses Gunn (Sergeant
Webster), Mario Van Peebles ('Stitch' Jones).

BIRD, Warner Brothers A Malpaso Production, USA, 1988
Director: Clint Eastwood
Forest Whitaker (Charlie 'Yardbird' Parker), Diane Venora
(Chan Richardson), Michael Zelniker (Red Rodney), Samuel E.
Wright (Dizzy Gillespie).

THE DEAD POOL, Warner Brothers A Malpaso Production,
USA, 1988
Director: Buddy Van Horn

Clint Eastwood (Inspector Harry Callahan), Patricia Clarkson (Samantha Walker), Liam Neeson (Peter Swan).

PINK CADILLAC, Malpaso for Warner Brothers, USA, 1989
Director: Buddy Van Horn
Clint Eastwood (Tommy Nowak), Bernadette Peters (Lou Ann McGuinn).

WHITE HUNTER, BLACK HEART, Malpaso/Rastar for Warner Brothers, USA, 1990
Director: Clint Eastwood
Clint Eastwood (John Wilson), Jeff Fahey (Peter Verrill), Charlotte Cornwell (Miss Wilding), Norman Lumsden (Butler George), George Dzundza (Paul Landers).

THE ROOKIE, Malpaso for Warner Brothers, USA, 1990
Director: Clint Eastwood
Clint Eastwood (Nick Pulovski), Charlie Sheen (David Ackerman), Raúl Julia (Strom), Sonia Braga (Liesel), Tom Skerritt (Eugene Ackerman), Lara Flynn Boyle (Sarah).

UNFORGIVEN, Malpaso/Warner Brothers, Alberta, Canada, 1992
Director: Clint Eastwood
Clint Eastwood (William Munny), Gene Hackman (Little Bill Dagget), Morgan Freeman (Ned Logan), Jaimz Woolvett (The Schofield Kid), Frances Fisher (Strawberry Alice), Saul Rubinek (Beauchamp), Richard Harris (English Bob).

Index